Text copyright © 2017 remains with the authors and for the collection with ATF Press. All rights reserved. Except for any fair dealing permitted under the Copyright Act, no part of the publication may be reproduced by any means without prior permission. Inquiries should be made in the first instance with the publisher.

Interface Theology:
Volume 3, Number 2, 2017

Editor Board
Revd Dr John Capper, University of Divinity, Melbourne
Dr Philip Kariatlis, St Andrews Greek Orthodox Theological College, Sydney

Editorial Manager
Mr Hilary Regan, Publisher, ATF Theology, PO Box 504 Hindmarsh. SA 5007, Australia. Fax +61 8 82235643.

International Reference Group
Rev Dr Vicky Balabanksi, Uniting College for Leadership and Theology, Adelaide
Rev Dr Ted Peters, Pacific Lutheran Theological School, Berkley
Rev Dr Murray Rae, University of Otago, Dunedin

Subscription rates
Print: Local: Individual Aus $55, Institutions Aus $65.
Overseas: Individuals US $60, Institutions US $65.

Interface Theology is a biannual refereed journal of theology published in print, epub and open access by ATF Press in Australia.
The journal is a scholarly ecumenical and interdisciplinary publication, aiming to serve the church and its mission, promoting a broad based interpretation of Christian theology within a trinitarian context, encouraging dialogue between Christianity and other faiths, and exploring the interface between faith and culture. It is published in English for an international audience.

ISSN 2203-465X
Cover design by Astrid Sengkey. Text Minion Pro Size 11

978-1-925872-00-2 soft
978-1-925872-01-9 hard
978-1-925872-02-6 epub
978-1-925872-03-3 pdf

An imprint of ATF Theology part of the ATF Press Publishing Group.
ATF (Australia) Ltd.
PO Box 504
Hindmarsh SA 5007
Australia
www.atfpress.com
Making a lasting impact

InterfaceTheology

Applied Ethics

Interface/Theology 3/2 2017

Table of Contents

---

1. The Law of Marriage Equality in Australia:
   The Shortest Distance Between Two Points?
   Megan Lawson and Paul Babie — 1

2. Action and Motive in Economic and Christian Ethics
   Geoffrey Brennan and Chris White — 31

The Law of Marriage Equality in Australia
The Shortest Distance Between Two Points?

Megan Lawson and Paul Babie*

Introduction

The world over, marriage, both as a legal institution and in its social practice, continues to evolve with changing socio-economic-political standards and mores.[1] As it changes it 'is becoming less hidebound, less dutiful and less obligatory—but even more important'.[2] One of the most significant developments in the global evolution of the legal institution of marriage concerns the emergence over the latter part of the twentieth century and into the twenty-first of equality for same-sex couples, or same-sex marriage. By varying means, over twenty nations have now legalised same-sex marriage.[3] The principal means by which this legalisation has occurred has been either through the decisions of courts or the enactment of legislatures to recognise the right to same sex marriage as a matter of fundamental equality.

---

*   Adelaide Law School, The University of Adelaide.
1. See, for example John Witte, Jr, *From Sacrament to Contract: Marriage, Religion, and Law in the Western Tradition* (Westminster John Knox Press, 2nd ed, 2012); Paul Babie, 'Synthesis or Separation? Church, State and Marriage in Byzantine Law', in *Journal of Law and Religion* 26 (2011): 585.
2. Joel Budd, 'A looser knot' in *The Economist, Special Report: Marriage* (25 November 2017): 3.
3. To date, countries where same-sex marriage is legal are: The Netherlands, Belgium, Canada, Spain, South Africa, Norway, Sweden, Argentina, Portugal, Iceland, Denmark, Uruguay, Brazil, France, England/Wales, New Zealand, Luxembourg, Scotland, United States, Ireland, Luxembourg, Finland, Slovenia, Colombia, Greenland and Australia: Ben Windsor, *Same-Sex Marriage Around the World: How Many Countries Have Legalised It?* (7 December 2017) SBS News <http://www.sbs.com.au/news/article/2017/06/01/factbox-same-sex-marriage-around-world>.

Two major federal systems demonstrate both approaches: the judicial and legislative. In the United States, lawsuits brought in state courts found that the exclusion of such marriages violated the equal protection clauses of state constitutions; in 2015, the United States Supreme Court struck down all state bans on same-sex marriage for failure to comply with the federal Constitution, thereby securing national marriage equality.[4] In Canada, several provincial appellate court decisions held bans on marriage equality to violate the *Canadian Charter of Rights and Freedoms*.[5] In 2004, the Supreme Court of Canada found that the federal Parliament could legislate to establish same-sex marriage;[6] this cleared the way for the enactment in 2005 of the *Civil Marriage Act*, thereby defining marriage as between 'two persons'.[7]

As with much of its approach to the complex relationship between law, religion and individual rights,[8] a piecemeal, ad hoc, and, to put it simply, convoluted and messy approach also characterises Australia's journey towards marriage equality. While prior to its amendment the *Marriage Act 1961* (Cth) defined marriage as 'the union of a *man and a woman* to the exclusion of all others, voluntarily entered into for life',[9] an increasing proportion of Australians have for some time favoured altering this definition to include same-sex couples.[10] Opponents, though, argue that such a redefinition is profoundly unjust to those who conscientiously believe, whether for religious or other reasons,

---

4. Adam Liptak, 'Supreme Court to Decide Marriage Rights for Gay Couples Nationwide', *New York Times* (online), 16 January 2015 <https://www.nytimes.com/2015/01/17/us/supreme-court-to-decide-whether-gays-nationwide-can-marry.html>.
5. *Halpern v Canada (Attorney-General)* (2003) 225 DLR (4th) 529.
6. *Reference re Same-Sex Marriage* (2004) 246 DLR (4th) 193.
7. *Civil Marriage Act*, SC 2005, c C-33.
8. See, for examle Paul Babie and Neville Rochow, 'Feels Like Déjà vu: Religious Freedom under a Proposed Australian Bill of Rights' (2010) *BYU Law Review* 821; Paul Babie, 'National Security and the Free Exercise Guarantee of Section 116: Time for a Judicial Interpretive Update', in *Federal Law Review,* 45 (2017): 351.
9. *Marriage Act 1961* (Cth) ('*Marriage Act*') (emphasis added).
10. Ronald Sackville, 'Law and Justice: Do They Meet—Some Personal Reflections', in *UNSW Law Journal,* 37 (2014): 1142, 1163.

that the institution of marriage should be confined to heterosexual relationships.[11] Strongly partisan views on both sides of this debate[12] raise political, social, religious, and moral questions.[13]

In light of these global shifts and domestic attitudes, on 9 August 2017, the Commonwealth Treasurer directed the Australian Bureau of Statistics (ABS) to conduct the Australian Marriage Law Postal Survey in order to collect information on the proportion of participating electors who are in favour of, and who oppose, the law being changed to allow same-sex couples to marry via post.[14] To finance this, the Minister for Finance issued an 'advance' of $122 million pursuant to the *Appropriation Act (No1) 2017- 2018* (Cth). This was then challenged in the High Court of Australia, and in considering both the direction and the advance, confirmed the validity of the postal survey, which the ABS then distributed to 16 million Australians.[15] Of the 79.5% of eligible Australians who responded,[16] an 'overwhelming' 61.6% voted 'yes' to the question 'should the law be changed to allow same-sex couples to marry?'.[17]

---

11. Sackville, 'Law and Justice: Do They Meet—Some Personal Reflections', 1142, 1163.
12. Mary Anne Neilsen, *Same-sex Marriage*, Parliamentary Library Briefing Book 44th Parliament Law and Bills Digest, December 2013 <https://www.aph.gov.au/About_Parliament/Parliamentary_Departments/Parliamentary_Library/pubs/BriefingBook44p/Marriage>.
13. Mary Anne Neilsen, *Same-sex Marriage*, Parliamentary Library Briefing Book 44th Parliament Law and Bills Digest, December 2013 <https://www.aph.gov.au/About_Parliament/Parliamentary_Departments/Parliamentary_Library/pubs/BriefingBook44p/Marriage>.
14. Australian Bureau Statistics, *Australian Marriage Law Postal Survey, 2017* (11 December 2017) Australian Bureau Statistics <http://www.abs.gov.au/ausstats/abs@.nsf/mf/1800.0>.
15. Gabrielle Appleby, *High Court Dismisses Challenge, So Australia Is Off To The (Postal) Polls On Same-Sex Marriage* (7 September 2017) The Conversation <https://theconversation.com/high-court-dismisses-challenge-so-australia-is-off-to-the-postal-polls-on-same-sex-marriage-82372>.
16. Of the eligible voting population, 12.6 million Australians submitted a clear response, 36,686 submitted a response that was not clear, and 3.2 million did not respond.
17. Australian Bureau Statistics, *National Results* (11 December 2017) Australian Bureau Statistics <http://www.abs.gov.au/ausstats/abs@.nsf/Lookup/by%20Subject/1800.0~2017~Main%20Features~Results~8>.

In the absence of any constitutionally implied right to equality[18] as found in the United States or Canada,[19] same-sex marriage is only possible through legislation enacted by the Commonwealth government.[20] In 2013, in *Commonwealth v Australian Capital Territory*,[21] the High Court held state or territory marriage equality legislation to be inoperative as being inconsistent with the Commonwealth's power to legislate in respect of marriage, that power having been exercised, thereby covering the field, with the enactment of the *Marriage Act 1961* (Cth).[22] Thus, following the survey result, having committed the Liberal government to acting upon the survey outcome, Prime Minister Malcolm Turnbull announced prompt amendment of the *Marriage Act 1961* (Cth) so as to enable same-sex couples to marry.[23]

While the survey result and the Prime Minister's commitment bring Australia a step closer to marriage equality, the ongoing political debate surrounding amendments seems to be producing the convoluted messiness that we have come to expect in attempting to mediate the relationship between religion and state.[24] Nonetheless, on 15 November, Senator Dean Smith introduced in the Senate the

---

18. Geoffrey Lindell, 'Constitutional Issues Regarding Same-Sex Marriage: A Comparative Survey — North America and Australasia' (2008) 30 *Sydney Law Review* 27, 37. See *Kruger v Commonwealth* (1997) 190 CLR 1. Cf *Leeth v Commonwealth* (1992) 174 CLR 455.
19. *United States Constitution* amend XIV; *Canadian Charter of Rights and Freedoms* s 15.
20. Lindell, above n 18, 38; Shipra Chordia, 'The High Court Same-Sex Marriage and Federalism' (2014) 39 *Alternative Law Journal* 84, 84; Anne Twomey, 'Same-Sex Marriage and Constitutional Interpretation', in *Australian Law Journal*, 88 (9) (2014): 613, 616.
21. *Commonwealth v Australian Capital Territory* (2013) 250 CLR 441 ('*Same-Sex Marriage Case*').
22. *Same-Sex Marriage Case* (2013) 250 CLR 469 [61].
23. Joe Kelly and Greg Brown 'Same-sex marriage vote result live: Yes vote wins, Brandis brokers deal with conservatives' *The Australian* (online), 15 November 2017 <https://sslcam.news.com.au/cam/authorise?channel=pc&url=http%3a%2f%2fwww.theaustralian.com.au%2fnational-affairs%2fsamesex-marriage-result-live-vote-details-news-opinion%2fnews-story%2f453863f06bad272ad58b9c8c8d4a8f88>.
24. Louise Yaxley, 'Same-Sex Marriage: Push to Let Florists and Bakers Discriminate Against Gay Weddings Dropped', *ABC News* (online) 27 November 2017 <http://www.abc.net.au/news/2017-11-27/push-dropped-to-let-florists-and-bakers-discriminate-ssm/9197448>.

Marriage Amendment (Definition and Religious Freedoms) Bill 2017 (Cth);[25] the bill was passed by the Senate on 29 November 2017.[26] The Bill received Royal Assent on 9 December 2017, and entered into force as the *Marriage Amendment (Definition and Religious Freedoms) Act 2017* (Cth) (*MAA*). Still, the fact that 17 bills dealing with same-sex marriage have been introduced in the Commonwealth Parliament since 2004,[27] the speed with which the government acted following the results of the postal survey does not obviate the truth that travelling the short distance between amendment and marriage equality is proving to be anything but the straight line that represents the shortest distance between two points.

This chapter provides an overview of the legal issues involved in providing for marriage equality in the form of same-sex marriage in Australia. It contains five parts. Part II briefly explores the legalisation experience in two federal democracies similar to that of the Australian: the United States and Canada; this serves to identify the issues that might arise, in respect of the right to equality inherent in same-sex marriage itself and of countervailing rights or interests (largely those based upon religious grounds) implicated in the provision of marriage equality. Part III examines the Australian constitutional framework within which the legalisation of same-sex marriage must occur. Part IV traces the Australian journey towards equality, beginning with the postal survey of 2017, the proposed amending bill, and the means chosen for protecting the free exercise of religious belief and practice on the part of those opposed to same-sex marriage. Part V offers brief concluding reflections.

The experience of two federal constitutional democracies that share the common law tradition with Australia reveals how the legalisation of same-sex marriage can be achieved through judicial and through legislative means. The United States serves as an example of the former and Canada of the latter.

---

25. ABC News, 'Same-Sex Marriage Bill', *ABC News* (online), 16 November 2017 <http://www.abc.net.au/news/2017-11-16/full-text-dean-smith-same-sex-marriage-bill-speech/9157270>.
26. Parliament of Australia, *Marriage Amendment (Definition and Religious Freedoms) Bill 2017* (December 2017) Parliament of Australia <https://www.aph.gov.au/Parliamentary_Business/Bills_Legislation/Bills_Search_Results/Result?bId=s1099>.
27. Neilsen, above n 12.

Same-Sex Marriage In Similar Federal Democracies

Other federal constitutional democracies that share the common law tradition with Australia can provide guidance as to how the legalisation of same-sex marriage can be achieved through judicial and through legislative means. Here we briefly examine two such systems: the United States serves as an example of judicial establishment of same-sex marriage, while Canada demonstrates how that end can be achieved through legislation.

United States

In the United States, the states, rather than the federal government, enjoys the power to govern marriage.[28] As such, the licencing and recognition of same-sex marriages across the United States began with state court decisions holding that the failure to include same-sex couples in the definition of marriage violated the equal protection clauses of relevant state constitutions.[29] In some states, constitutional amendments followed, seeking either to prevent or to overturn such judicial innovation. This first occurred in 1993, in *Baehr v Lewin*,[30] in which the Supreme Court of Hawaii held that a legislative ban on same-sex marriage amounted to discrimination in violation of the equal protection guarantee of the state's constitution.[31] Following this decision, a constitutional amendment withdrew the application of the state equal protection guarantee, leaving the legislature free to ban same-sex marriages. In late 1999, the Supreme Court held that this new ban was effective and refused to recognise same-sex marriages.[32] Over the next decade, state courts followed the example first set by the Supreme Court of Hawaii in *Baehr v Lewin*, holding that the prohibition of same-sex marriage was converse to guarantees of equality in the respective state constitutions.[33]

---

28. *Hisquierdo v Hisquierdo*, 439 US 572 (1979); *United States v Windsor*, 570 US (2013).
29. Lindell, above n 18, 27.
30. *Baehr v Lewin* 852 P 2d 44 (Haw, 1993).
31. *Baehr v Lewin* 852 P 2d 44 (Haw, 1993).
32. *Baehr v Miilke*, 994 P 2d 566 (Haw, 1999).
33. Hawaii: *Baehr v Lewin*, 852 P 2d 44 (Haw, 1993); Vermont: *Baker v Vermont*, 744 A 2d 864 (Vt, 1999); Massachusetts: *Goodridge v Department of Public Health*, 798 NE 2d 941 (Mass, 2003) and *In re Opinions of the Justices to the Senate* 802 NE 2d 565 (Mass, 2004).

While some states took legislative action without first having been catalysed by the judiciary,[34] typically, the success of same-sex marriage in the states involved the interplay of judicial and legislative action. Thus, in 2003, the Supreme Judicial Court of Massachusetts found that laws excluding same-sex marriages violated the *Massachusetts Constitution* in failing to confer upon the members of same-sex relationships the same rights and benefits as those conferred upon heterosexual ones.[35] Chief Judge Margaret Marshall, writing for a 4-3 majority, observed that 'it is circular reasoning, not analysis, to maintain that marriage must remain a heterosexual institution because that is what it historically has been'[36] and accordingly reformulated the common law definition of marriage as being between 'two persons'.[37] The Court, however, suspended the effect of its declaration for 180 days so as to allow the legislature to act.[38] In response, the Senate drafted a bill providing for 'civil unions' between persons of the same sex. In an advisory opinion, the Supreme Judicial Court rejected this scheme,[39] indicating that it, too, violated the state equal protection guarantee, even though the partners to such a union would have enjoyed the same rights and duties as partners in a traditional marriage.[40] The Court wrote that '[t]he history of our nation has demonstrated that separate is seldom, if ever, equal'.[41] Following this, in May 2004, the legislature licensed and recognised same-sex marriage.[42]

And in May 2008, the Supreme Court of California, as had the Supreme Judicial Court of Massachusetts, held unconstitutional legislation banning same-sex marriage for 'discriminating on the basis of sexual orientation' in the same way as laws that discriminate by race or gender.[43] The Court found that Constitution of California protected the 'basic civil or human right of *all* people'— including

---

34. Michael Cole-Schwartz, *Mayor Adrian Fenty Signs DC Marriage Bill* (18 December 2009) HRC Backstory <https://web.archive.org/web/20110721114655/http://www.hrcbackstory.org/2009/12/mayor-adrian-fenty-signs-dc-marriage-bill/>.
35. *Goodridge v Department of Public Health*, 798 NE 2d 941, 967 (Mass, 2003).
36. *Goodridge v Department of Public Health*, 798 NE 2d 941, 961 n 23.
37. *Goodridge v Department of Public Health*, 798 NE 2d 941, 961 n 23.
38. *Goodridge v Department of Public Health*, 798 NE 964.
39. *In re Opinions of the Justices to the Senate* 802 NE 2d 565 (Mass, 2004).
40. *In re Opinions of the Justices to the Senate* 802 NE 2d 565 (Mass, 2004)..
41. *In re Opinions of the Justices to the Senate* 802 NE 2d 572.
42. *In re Opinions of the Justices to the Senate* 802 NE 2d 565 (Mass, 2004).
43. *Re Marriage Cases* 183 P 3d 384 (Cal, 2008).

same-sex couples — to marry.[44] Yet in November 2008, the voters of California followed their counterparts in twenty-two other states,[45] by approving constitutional amendments defining marriage as the union of one man and one woman. The *California Marriage Protection Act*, widely known as 'Proposition 8', entrenched the status of marriage in the state as between a 'man and a woman', reversing the judicial legalisation of same-sex marriage.[46] Following its enactment, two homosexual couples brought suit in the United States District Court; in 2010, in *Perry v Schwarzenegger*,[47] the court held Proposition 8 to violate the Due Process and the Equal Protection clauses of the US Constitution. As a result, the issuance of marriage licenses to same-sex couples in California resumed in June 2013.[48]

While the states hold the power to govern marriage, the federal government nonetheless had a part to play in what would ultimately result in the judicial recognition of same-sex marriage. In 1996, Congress enacted the *Defence of Marriage Act*, widely referred to as 'DOMA'. While it did not prohibit same-sex marriages, or require any state to prohibit them, it defined marriage as between one man and one woman. This had the effect of denying federal benefits to same-sex couples, and exempted states from recognising same-sex marriages performed in other states[49] so as to 'defend the institution of traditional heterosexual marriage'.[50] In other words, DOMA

---

44. *Re Marriage Cases* 183 P 3d 426.
45. In 2004, Arkansas, Georgia, Kentucky, Michigan, Mississippi, Montana, North Dakota, Ohio, Oklahoma, Oregon, Utah; in 2005, Alabama, Arizona, Colorado, Florida, Idaho, Kansas, South Carolina, South Dakota, Texas, Virginia and Wisconsin: Joel Roberts, '11 States Ban Same-Sex Marriage' *CBS News* (online) 30 September 2004 <https://www.cbsnews.com/news/11-states-ban-same-sex-marriage/>. As of January 2010, 29 states had constitutionally confined marriage to being between one man and one woman, while 12 others had statutes to this effect: *States Issue Verdict on Gay Rights, Abortion* (5 November 2008) NBC News <http://www.nbcnews.com/id/27523989/ns/politics-decision_08/>.
46. Jesse McKinley And Laurie Goodstein, 'Bans in 3 States on Gay Marriage', *New York Times* (online) 5 November 2008 <http://www.nytimes.com/2008/11/06/us/politics/06marriage.html>.
47. *Perry v Schwarzenegger* 704 F Supp 2d 921 (Cal, 2010).
48. Ed Pilkington and Eoin Reynolds, 'Same-sex marriages to resume in California after Prop 8 ruling' *The Guardian* (online) 26 July 2013 <https://www.theguardian.com/world/2013/jun/26/gay-marriage-california-prop-8-supreme-court>.
49. Deborah A Batts, 'Repeal DOMA' (2003) 30 *Human Rights* 2, 2.
50. Congressional House Report No 104-664, 2 (1996).

purported 'to *relieve* rather than *oblige* States' to recognise such marriages or unions.[51] In June 2013, the US Supreme Court struck down part of DOMA as unconstitutional for allowing inequality of benefits provided to those who resided in states where same-sex marriage was legal as compared to those who lived in states where it was not.[52] The majority held DOMA 'single[d] out a class of persons' and 'impose[d] a disability on the class' such that it instructs that a same-sex 'marriage is less worthy than the marriages of others'. This, the court found, violated the due process and equal protection guarantees of US *Constitution*.[53]

By July 2015, same-sex marriage was legal in thirty-seven states and the District of Columbia, but remained prohibited in thirteen states.[54] In light of this 'instability and uncertainty' caused by state marriage laws differing with regard to same-sex couples, the US Supreme Court agreed to hear *Obergefell v Hodges*, which consolidated four appeals challenging state laws that prohibited same-sex marriage in Michigan, Kentucky, Tennessee, and Ohio.[55] On 26 June 2015, the Court struck down all state bans on same-sex marriage, thus legalising it in all fifty states.[56] The majority found that the right to marriage equality was enshrined under the 14th amendment equal protection clause of the US Constitution.[57] Justice Kennedy, writing for the majority, observed:

> No union is more profound than marriage, for it embodies the highest ideals of love, fidelity, devotion, sacrifice, and family
> ...
> It would misunderstand these men and women to say they disrespect the idea of marriage. Their plea is that they do

---

51. Lindell, above n 18, 47.
52. *United States v Windsor*, 570 US (2013).
53. *United States v Windsor*, 570 US (2013) 29.
54. Julia Zorthian, 'These States are Where SCOTUS Just legalized Same-sex Marriage' *Time* (online) 26 June 2015 <http://time.com/3937662/gay-marriage-supreme-court-states-legal/>
55. *Obergefell v Hodges* 556 US 28 (2015), consolidated with *DeBoer v Snyder* (14-571), *Tanco v Haslam* (14-562), *Bourke v Beshear* (14-574).
56. Zorthian, above n 54.
57. Jesse McKinley And Laurie Goodstein, 'Bans in 3 States on Gay Marriage', *New York Times* (online) 5 November 2008 <https://www.nytimes.com/2015/01/17/us/supreme-court-to-decide-whether-gays-nationwide-can-marry.html>.

respect it, respect it so deeply that they seek to find its fulfillment for themselves. Their hope is not to be condemned to live in loneliness, excluded from one of civilization's oldest institutions. *They ask for equal dignity in the eyes of the law. The Constitution grants them that right.*[58]

Accordingly, the Court held all state same-sex marriage bans unconstitutional. All 50 states now issue marriage licenses to same-sex couples and recognise such marriages validly performed in other jurisdictions.[59] The legalisation of same-sex marriage in the United States began with the courts, relied upon the interplay of judicial and legislative action, and ultimately relied upon judicial pronouncement for its national recognition.

Canada

In Canada, it is the national government, and not the provinces (the equivalent of American and Australian states) that enjoy the power to legislate in respect of marriage.[60] This constitutional difference notwithstanding, like the American experience, the federal Parliament of Canada reacted to judicial decisions finding bans on same-sex marriage unconstitutional; unlike the American experience, though, the Parliament took initial steps to legalise same-sex marriage, but acted only once the Supreme Court of Canada validated the constitutionality of such action. In the final result, the national legislature, and not the high court, established same-sex marriage. Thus, in 2005, Canada became the first country outside of Europe to legalise same-sex marriage, with the federal Parliament enacting legislation after four Court of Appeal rulings legalised the practice in the majority of the country's provinces.[61]

---

58. *Obergefell v Hodges* 556 US 28 (2015) (emphasis added).
59. *Obergefell v Hodges* 556 US 28 (2015).
60. *Constitution Act* 1867 (UK) s 91(26) which gives the Dominion Parliament exclusive power to legislate with respect to 'Marriage and Divorce' and compare s 92(12) which gives the legislatures of the Provinces exclusive power to legislate with respect to the 'The Solemnization of Marriage in the Province'.
61. *EGALE Canada Inc v Attorney-General (Canada)* (2003) 13 BCLR (4th) 1; *Halpern (Attorney-General) (Canada)* (2003) 65 OR (3d) 161; *Hendricks c Procureur Général* (Québec) [2002] RJQ 2506; *Dunbar v Yukon* (2004) 122 CRR (2d) 149.

In 2003, for instance, the Ontario Court of Appeal held that laws prohibiting same-sex marriages perpetuated a view that same-sex couples are less capable or worthy of recognition or value as human beings; this contravened the guarantee of equality contained in s 15(1) of the *Canadian Charter of Rights and Freedoms*.[62] Accordingly, the definition of marriage was invalid to the extent that it referred to a union between 'one man and one woman' and was reformulated to refer to 'two persons'[63] since '... the term "marriage" has the constitutional flexibility necessary to meet changing realities of Canadian society without the need for recourse to constitutional amendment procedures.'[64]

Following this decision, the Canadian Parliament posed a reference case to the Supreme Court of Canada seeking definition of the national Parliament's power to legislate for same-sex marriage. In *Reference re Same-Sex Marriage*,[65] the Court emphasised that it was insufficient to show that historically and according to religious beliefs marriage was inherently limited to opposite-sex relationships.[66] Rather, the *Charter* as 'a living tree which, by way of progressive interpretation, accommodates and addresses the realities of modern life', requires that same-sex marriage be recognised so as to comply with the equality provision of s 15(1).[67]

The legislative power to do so thus confirmed, in 2005, the Canadian Parliament enacted uniform national legislation codifying the definition of marriage for the first time as being between 'two persons'.[68] The *Civil Marriage Act* states that it is only by allowing same-sex couples equally to access the institution of marriage that their rights to equality without discrimination can be respected.[69]

---

62. *Halpern v Canada (Attorney-General)* (2003) 225 DLR (4th) 529 (Ontario Court of Appeal) 554–562 [77]–[108].
63. *Halpern v Canada (Attorney-General)* (2003) 225 DLR (4th) 529 (Ontario Court of Appeal) 569–572 [143]–[154].
64. *Halpern v Canada (Attorney-General)* (2003) 225 DLR (4th) 529 (Ontario Court of Appeal) 547 [46].
65. (2004) 246 DLR (4th) 193 (British Columbia Court of Appeal).
66. *Reference re Same-Sex Marriage* (2004) 246 DLR (4th) 193 (British Columbia Court of Appeal) 553 [71].
67. *Reference re Same-Sex Marriage* (2004) 246 DLR (4th) 193 (British Columbia Court of Appeal) 204 [22]; Lindell, above n 18, 40, n 62.
68. *Civil Marriage Act*, SC 2005, c C-33.
69. *Civil Marriage Act*, SC 2005, c C-33.

Unlike the United States and Canada, Australia enjoys no comprehensive constitutional protection for equality and to be free from discrimination.[70] As such, while the courts might provide guidance in relation to the constitutional power in respect of marriage, they can do nothing in respect of the validity of exercises of that power relative to equality and non-discrimination principles. We turn now to the Australian constitutional framework for establishing same-sex marriage.

Constitutional Framework

The American and Canadian experiences illustrate how a constitutionally-enshrined right to equality[71] or a general prohibition on the enactment of discriminatory legislation[72] influences the judicial consideration and ultimate legalisation of same-sex marriage. Australia has no such constitutional protections and,[73] as such, any recognition of same-sex marriage must depend upon the power of government— either Commonwealth/territory or state—to legislate for such recognition.[74] Or, put another way, while '[p]arliament can legislate on this matter [marriage] under the federal distribution of legislative powers — [the courts have no power to assess the] outcome that results from that distribution'.[75]

It is necessary, then, to determine whether it is the Commonwealth or the states and territories that enjoy the power to legislate with respect to same-sex marriage. Section 51(xxi) of the *Consti-*

---

70. National Human Rights Action Plan, *Equality and Non-Discrimination Laws* (2011) National Human Rights Action Plan <http://www.humanrightsactionplan.org.au/nhrap/focus-area/equality-and-non-discrimination-laws>.
71. Lindell, above n 18, 37. See *Kruger v Commonwealth* (1997) 190 CLR 1. Cf *Leeth v Commonwealth* (1992) 174 CLR 455.
72. Lindell, above n 18, 42.
73. National Human Rights Action Plan, *Equality and Non-Discrimination Laws* (2011) National Human Rights Action Plan <http://www.humanrightsactionplan.org.au/nhrap/focus-area/equality-and-non-discrimination-laws>.
74. National Human Rights Action Plan, *Equality and Non-Discrimination Laws* (2011) National Human Rights Action Plan, 38 <http://www.humanrightsactionplan.org.au/nhrap/focus-area/equality-and-non-discrimination-laws>; Chordia, above n 20, 84.
75. Lindell, above n 18, 58.

tution provides that the Commonwealth Parliament has power to make laws with respect to 'marriage', which it has exercised in enacting the *Marriage Act 1961* (Cth). Two related questions emerge. First, does the power in s 51(xxi) extend only to 'traditional' heterosexual marriage, or has its constitutional meaning evolved so as to encompass legislating for same-sex marriage? Or, second, is it possible that the marriage power is concurrent, thereby allowing *both* the Commonwealth *and* the territories and states to make laws regarding marriage, with only inconsistent state or territory laws giving way (to the extent of the inconsistency)[76] to the *Marriage Act 1961* (Cth)? Indeed, in attempting to enact laws with respect to same-sex marriage, New South Wales, Tasmania, Western Australia, South Australia and the Australian Capital Territory have all taken this latter position.[77] The High Court resolved both questions in its 2013 decision in *Commonwealth v Australian Capital Territory*,[78] in which the Commonwealth challenged the constitutionality of the Australian Capital Territory's attempt to legislate for same-sex marriage in the *Marriage Equality (Same Sex) Act 2013* (ACT) ('*ACT Act*').

The *ACT Act* enabled same-sex marriages to be conducted and recognised in the Australian Capital Territory; while it defined 'marriage' as 'the union of *2 people of the same sex* to the exclusion of all others, voluntarily entered into for life', the *ACT Act* specifically excluded 'marriage' within the meaning of the *Marriage Act 1961* (Cth).[79] The Commonwealth argued that the *ACT Act* established a definition of marriage inconsistent with the *Marriage Act 1961* (Cth), contrary to s 28 of the *Australian Capital Territory (Self-Government) Act 1988* (Cth); and, importantly, the paramountcy provision in s 109 of the *Constitution* could not apply as this case involved territory,

---

76. *Australian Constitution* s 109; *Australian Capital Territory (Self-Government) Act 1988* s 28(1).
77. Same-Sex Marriage Bill 2012 (Tas); Same-Sex Marriage Bill 2013 (NSW); Marriage Equality Bill 2012 (Vic); Same Sex Marriage Bill 2013 (SA); Same-Sex Marriage Bill 2013 (WA).
78. (2013) 250 CLR 441.
79. *Same-Sex Marriage Case* (2013) 250 CLR 441, 46 [55], 468 [60].

rather than state, legislation.[80] The ACT submitted no inconsistency existed in the relevant sense: the *Marriage Act 1961* (Cth) provided for the marriage of heterosexual couples while the *ACT Act* established marriage for same-sex couples. Thus, no direct conflict arose between the Commonwealth and ACT laws. Rather, the ACT argued, as with state legislation providing for de facto relationships,[81] the two operated concurrently.[82]

The High Court, however, acting with uncharacteristic speed,[83] unanimously struck down the *ACT Act*.[84] The Court began with 2004 amendments to the *Marriage Act 1961* (Cth),[85] which, in the words of the Minister's second reading speech, were designed 'to provide certainty to all Australians about the meaning of marriage in the future'[86] by ensuring that 'same sex relationships cannot be equated with marriage'.[87] These amendments expressly inserted a definition of marriage as that between 'a man and a woman',[88] and prohibited

---

80. This is similar to s 109 of the *Constitution,* however that section only applies to conflicts between federal and state laws. The *Australian Capital Territory (Self-Government) Act 1988* s 28(1):

    A provision of an enactment has no effect to the extent that it is inconsistent with [an ACT law], but such a provision shall be taken to be consistent with such a law to the extent that it is capable of operating concurrently with that law.

81. Lindell, above n 18, 43.
82. Australian Capital Territory, 'Annotated Submissions of the Australian Capital Territory', Submission in *Commonwealth v Australian Capital Territory*, 25 November 2013, 3-6.
83. Michael Kirby, 'The ACT Marriage Equality Case - Losing the Battle but Winning the Constitutional War' (2016) 18 *Southern Cross University Law Review* 79, 88.
84. French CJ, Hayne, Crennan, Kiefel, Bell and Keane JJ. Gageler J excused himself presumably because as former Solicitor-General had many years earlier advised the ACT government on the legality of a Territorian scheme for the marriage-like recognition of unions between people of the same sex: Brad Jessup, 'Over the Summer: Same Sex Marriage and Gay Sex Criminal Records' (2014) 39(1) *Alternative Law Journal* 52, 58.
85. *Marriage Amendment Act 2004* (Cth).
86. Commonwealth, *Parliamentary Debates*, House of Representatives, 24 June 2004 (Philip Ruddock) at 31460 and Senate, 12 August 2004 (Ian MacDonald) at 26504 and see also at 26555.
87. Explanatory Memorandum, *Marriage Amendment Act 2004* (Cth), General Outline.
88. *Marriage Act 1961* (Cth) s 5(1).

the recognition of same-sex marriages solemnised overseas.[89] Having determined that 'the kind of marriage provided for by the [*Marriage Act 1961* (Cth)] is the *only* kind of marriage that may be formed or recognised in Australia', the High Court concluded that the Commonwealth Parliament's intention was exhaustively to cover the field of all forms of marriage, leaving no room for a territory law to operate concurrently with the Commonwealth on that field.[90]

The Court found that the object of the *ACT Act*, however, was:

> to provide for marriage *equality* for same sex couples, not for some form of legally recognised relationship which is relevantly different from the relationship of marriage which the federal laws provide for and recognise.[91]

The 'thrust and purpose' of the *ACT Act* was marriage equality,[92] and that was inconsistent with the 'single and indivisible' statement of the law of marriage contained in the *Marriage Act 1961* (Cth). The *ACT Act* was thus inoperative and of 'no effect'.[93] Moreover, in purporting to operate on that field, the *ACT Act* was inconsistent with the *Marriage Act 1961* (Cth), and therefore rendered inoperative by s 28 of the *Australian Capital Territory (Self-Government) Act 1988* (Cth).

While the conclusion of irreconcilable inconsistency rendered it 'strictly unnecessary' to contemplate whether the Commonwealth possessed the power to provide for same-sex marriage, the Court nonetheless considered whether the scope of the Commonwealth marriage power might extend to same-sex marriage.[94] The issue turned on the fact that 'the ACT Act would probably operate concurrently with the *Marriage Act* if the federal Parliament had no power

---

89. *Marriage Act 1961* (Cth) s 88EA.
90. Geoffrey Lindell, 'State Legislative Power to Enact Same-Sex Marriage Legislation, and the Effect of The *Marriage Act 1961* (Cth) as amended by the *Marriage Amendment Act 2004* (Cth)' (2006) 9(2) *Constitutional Law and Policy Review* 25, 2.
91. *Same-Sex Marriage Case* (2013) 250 CLR 441, 452 [3].
92. Dan Meagher, 'Commonwealth v Australian Capital Territory' (2014) 25 *Public Law Review* 157, 159.
93. *Same-Sex Marriage Case* (2013) 250 CLR 441, 467 [55].
94. Chordia, above n 20, 84.

to make a national law providing for same sex marriage.'[95] Did the Commonwealth enjoy legislative power in respect of same-sex marriage? In providing an answer, the Court explicitly eschewed a definition merely because it 'accord[ed] with a preconceived notion of what marriage "should" be'[96] and that which might be based upon the original and contemporary meaning of marriage.[97] Instead, the Court examined changes to marriage throughout history. In so doing, the Court highlighted the fact that the social institution of marriage changes over time—and that the rights and obligations attached to the status of marriage 'never have been, and are not now, immutable'.[98] Accordingly, the Court found that the meaning of marriage in the constitutional context constituted a juristic concept lacking precise demarcation.[99] Rather, that meaning ought to be interpreted broadly so as to ensure that the constitutional power adapts to new cultural and social developments,[100] perhaps unforeseen by the framers,[101] and by reference to the scope of marriage as found in other legal systems.[102] On that basis, the Court defined 'marriage' for the purpose of s 51(xxi) of the *Constitution* as:

> a consensual union formed between natural persons in accordance with legally prescribed requirements which is not only a union the law recognises as intended to endure and be terminable only in accordance with law but also a union to which the law accords a status affecting and defining mutual rights and obligations.[103]

---

95. *Same-Sex Marriage Case* (2013) 250 CLR 441, 454 [9]; Stephen Puttick, 'All-Embracing Approaches to Constitutional Interpretation & Moderate Originalism' (2017) 42 *University of Western Australia Law Review* 30, 38 n 35; Twomey, above n 20, 613.
96. *Same-Sex Marriage Case* (2013) 250 CLR 441, 462 [36].
97. *Same-Sex Marriage Case* (2013) 250 CLR 455 [14]; Puttick, above n 95, 38.
98. *Same-Sex Marriage Case* (2013) 250 CLR 441, 456 [16].
99. Citing *Attorney-General (Vic) v Commonwealth (Marriage Act Case)* (1962) 107 CLR 529, 543 (Dixon CJ), 576–80 (Windeyer J).
100. *Same-sex Marriage Case* (2013) 250 CLR 441, 456 [17]-[19].
101. Lindell, above n 18, 38–9.
102. *Same-Sex Marriage Case* (2013) 250 CLR 441, 459 [22].
103. *Same-Sex Marriage Case* (2013) 250 CLR [33].

And, as such, the marriage power could embrace 'a marriage between persons of the same sex';[104] the Commonwealth therefore has the ability to legislate to enact same-sex marriage.[105] Nonetheless, '[s]o long as the *Marriage Act* continued to define "marriage" as it now does' the *ACT Act* was inoperative, and weddings conducted pursuant the *ACT Act* had 'no effect'.[106]

The High Court's reasoning in the *Same-Sex Marriage Case* meant that while it was theoretically possible to do so,[107] any attempt by a state or territory to legislate for same-sex marriage, such a statute would almost certainly be inconsistent with the *Marriage Act 1961* (Cth) and therefore invalid to the extent of that inconsistency.[108] Much more importantly, however, the outcome in the *Same-Sex Marriage Case* meant that the 'proponents of marriage equality . . . lost the battle to uphold the Territory law' but won the 'war'.[109] The result, in other words, rendered it 'undoubtedly clear' that the concept of marriage is not necessarily limited to heterosexual couples, and that the Commonwealth possessed the power to enact uniform national legislation providing for same-sex marriage.[110] Put another way, the outcome in the *Same-Sex Marriage Case* converted same-sex marriage from a matter of law to a 'political choice' as to the exercise of the marriage power to provide for same-sex marriage.[111] As we will see, exercising that choice proved to be far from a straightforward matter of the shortest distance between two points, one being the decision to allow for same-sex marriage, and the other being the legislation providing for it.

An Australian Journey

The Constitutional framework for such a change established as a matter of political choice, the Commonwealth Parliament set out on its

---

104. *Same-Sex Marriage Case* (2013) 250 CLR 462 [37]; Sackville, above n 10, 1163 n 71; Lindell, above n 18, 40.
105. Twomey, above n 20, 613; Jessup, above n 84, 58.
106. *Same-Sex Marriage Case* (2013) 250 CLR 44, 466 [53]. See George Williams, 'Same-Sex Marriage and the Australian States' (2015) 40(1) *Alternative Law Journal* 4, 4.
107. Chordia, above n 20, 84.
108. Williams, above n 106, 7, 8; Meagher, above n 92, 160.
109. Kirby, above n 83, 91.
110. Kirby, above n 83, 91; Chordia, above n 20, 84.
111. Twomey, above n 20, 616; Chordia, above n 20, 84.

journey towards exercising that choice precedent to legislating for national marriage equality. Yet, as with so much of the Australian approach to mediating the relationship between equality and religion, that journey has been, at best, convoluted and, at worst, messy. In this Part we examine three dimensions of that convolutedness/messiness: the decision to condition the exercise of the Commonwealth's legislative power concerning marriage upon a postal survey; the amendments to the *Marriage Act 1961* (Cth) ultimately enacted in the *Marriage Amendment (Definition and Religious Freedoms) Act 2017* (Cth); and, the implications for religious freedom in so legislating for same-sex marriage.

Postal Survey

Interestingly, the postal survey used by the Commonwealth government to condition its legislative power over marriage in the case of same-sex marriage implicated all three branches of government. The Executive and legislative branches issued a directive and advance for the implementation of the postal survey, while the High Court confirmed the constitutionality of that approach. We consider each of those interventions in turn.

1. Directive and Advance

In mid-2015, then Prime Minister Tony Abbott promised a plebiscite on the issue of same-sex marriage.[112] The first attempt to fulfill that promise involved the introduction of the *Plebiscite (Same-Sex Marriage) Bill 2016* (Cth), which was defeated twice by the Senate in November 2016 and again in August 2017. A compulsory plebiscite having failed,[113] the Commonwealth, now under the Turnbull Government, opted for a 'voluntary postal plebiscite' or postal survey.

---

112. ABC News, *Fact Check: Is the Same-Sex Marriage Survey a Completely Novel Idea That is Not Actually a Plebiscite?* (29 August 2017) ABC <http://www.abc.net.au/news/2017-08-22/fact-check-same-sex-marriage-postal-survey/8826300>.
113. ABC News, *Fact Check: Is the Same-Sex Marriage Survey a Completely Novel Idea That is Not Actually a Plebiscite?*.

To be conducted by the Australian Bureau of Statistics (ABS),[114] this option would allow the ABS to utilise its statutory power to request information from electors; here, that power would be used to gather information as to whether the law should be changed to allow same-sex couples to marry.[115]

In August 2017, the Commonwealth took two steps in furtherance of the postal survey. First, the Treasurer issued the Census and Statistics (Statistical Information) Direction 2017' ('the Direction'), thereby directing the ABS to collect information on the proportion of electors who agree or disagree that the law should be changed to allow same-sex couples to marry. Pursuant to the Direction, the ABS sought the assistance of the Australian Electoral Commission ('AEC') to conduct a postal survey so as to gather the relevant information.[116]

Second, in order to fund the Directive, the Finance Minister issued a determination entitled 'Advance to the Finance Minister Determination (No 1 of 2017–2018)' ('the Determination') to provide the ABS with $122 million. The Determination was made pursuant to s 10 of the *Appropriation Act (No1) 2017- 2018* (Cth), which allows the Minister to make a determination to provide for expenditures not exceeding $295 million where 'satisfied that there is an *urgent need* for expenditure, in the current year, that is not provided for ... because the expenditure was *unforeseen* until after the last on which it was practicable to provide for it [in the original Bill]'.[117] The Minister was purportedly satisfied that an 'urgent need' existed on the basis that the 2017–18 budget was tabled in May 2017, and that the policy to direct the ABS to conduct the survey had not changed until August.

2. Constitutional Validity

On 10 August 2017, two proceedings commenced challenging the Direction and the Determination. Andrew Wilkie, an independent Member of the House of Representatives, Felicity Marlowe, an elector

---

114. ABC News, *Fact Check: Is the Same-Sex Marriage Survey a Completely Novel Idea That is Not Actually a Plebiscite?*.
115. *Wilkie v The Commonwealth, Australian Marriage Equality Ltd v Cormann* (2017) 349 ALR 1, 9 [26].
116. *Wilkie v The Commonwealth, Australian Marriage Equality Ltd v Cormann* (2017) 349 ALR 112 [45]
117. *Appropriation Act (No1) 2017- 2018* (Cth) s 10 (emphasis added).

in a de facto relationship with a woman, and PFLAG Brisbane Inc, an association comprised of parents and friends of gay and lesbian people brought the first action,[118] seeking declarations and injunctions against the Commonwealth, the Finance Minister, the Treasurer, the Australian Statistician and the Electoral Commissioner.[119] Writs of prohibition were also sought against the Australian Statistician, preventing him from expending the amount in the Determination and from carrying out the Direction.[120] The plaintiffs alleged that (i) s 10 of the *Appropriation Act (No1) 2017- 2018* (Cth) was constitutionally invalid or, alternatively, that the Determination was invalid because it was not authorised by that section; (ii) the Direction was not authorised pursuant to s 9(1)(b) of the *Census and Statistics Act* 1905 (Cth); and, (iii) that the AEC was not authorised by s 7A of the *Electoral Act* 1918 (Cth) to assist the ABS.

Australian Marriage Equality Ltd, which advocates for the legalisation of marriage between consenting adults irrespective of gender, and Senator Janet Rice, a Senator for the State of Victoria and a member of the Australian Greens, commenced the second action. These plaintiffs contended solely that the Determination was not authorised by s 10 of *Appropriation Act*. Because s 10 of *Appropriation Act* formed the central focus of the challenge in both proceedings,[121] resulting in overlap of the claims,[122] the High Court heard both proceedings together. Ultimately, the Court unanimously dismissed both proceedings.[123]

---

118. *Wilkie v The Commonwealth, Australian Marriage Equality Ltd v Cormann* (2017) 349 ALR 1, 13 [48].
119. *Wilkie v The Commonwealth, Australian Marriage Equality Ltd v Cormann* (2017) 349 ALR 1 13 [49].
120. *Wilkie v The Commonwealth, Australian Marriage Equality Ltd v Cormann* (2017) 349 ALR 1 13 [49].
121. *Wilkie v The Commonwealth, Australian Marriage Equality Ltd v Cormann* (2017) 349 ALR 1 8 [23].
122. *Wilkie v The Commonwealth, Australian Marriage Equality Ltd v Cormann* (2017) 349 ALR 1 14 [54].
123. Gabrielle Appleby, *High Court Dismisses Challenge, So Australia is Off to the (Postal) Polls on Same-Sex Marriage* (7 September 2017) The Conversation <https://theconversation.com/high-court-dismisses-challenge-so-australia-is-off-to-the-postal-polls-on-same-sex-marriage-82372>.

As a preliminary matter, the defendants raised the issue of standing, arguing that the plaintiffs lacked sufficiency of interest.[124] In the result, however, the Court found it 'inappropriate to address' standing, given that the substantive challenges would have failed in any event.[125] As such, the Court considered: (i) the constitutionality of s 10 of the *Appropriation Act (No1) 2017- 2018* (Cth); (ii) whether the Commonwealth had failed to satisfy the criterion in that section, thereby failing to enliven the Minister's power to issue the Determination; (iii) the validity of the Direction; and, (iv) the permissibility of the AEC's assistance. We briefly consider each of those issues.

(a). *Appropriation Act (No1) 2017–2018* (Cth)

When read together, sections 81 and 83 of the *Constitution* provide that 'that no money can be taken out of the consolidated Fund . . . excepting under a distinct authorization from Parliament itself'.[126] The plaintiffs in both challenges to the Direction alleged that the Government had contravened this constitutional limit by impermissibly delegating the power to appropriate to the Finance Minister through s 10 of the *Appropriation Act (No1) 2017- 2018* (Cth).[127]

Having reviewed the history of appropriations legislation, the Court rejected as based on a 'fundamental misconstruction'[128] the contention that appropriations, whether special or annual, are permissible only for a purpose that has been determined by Parliament.[129] Rather, the Court found, s 12 of the *Appropriation Act (No1) 2017-2018* (Cth) operates to appropriate monies from the Consolidated Revenue Fund not when those monies are paid, but when the *Appro-*

---

124. *Wilkie v The Commonwealth, Australian Marriage Equality Ltd v Cormann* (2017) 349 ALR 1, 14 [56]–[58].
125. *Wilkie v The Commonwealth, Australian Marriage Equality Ltd v Cormann* (2017) 349 ALR 1, 14 [56]–[59].
126. *Brown v West* (1990) 169 CLR 195, 205, 208 quoting *Auckland Harbour Board v The King* [1924] AC 318, 326 [61].
127. *Wilkie v The Commonwealth, Australian Marriage Equality Ltd v Cormann* (2017) 349 ALR 1, 18 [72].
128. *Wilkie v The Commonwealth, Australian Marriage Equality Ltd v Cormann* (2017) 349 ALR 1, 21 [87].
129. *Wilkie v The Commonwealth, Australian Marriage Equality Ltd v Cormann* (2017) 349 ALR 1, 16 [64].

priation Act (No1) 2017- 2018 (Cth) itself commences.[130] Accordingly, $295 million was appropriated in the same way as the whole of the annual Commonwealth budget,[131] and could later be allocated via s 10. Thus, the Finance Minister's power here involved the allocation of money *already* appropriated by Parliament.[132]

(b). Determination

The plaintiffs also argued a failure to meet the precondition to the exercise of power set out in s 10(1) of the *Appropriation Act (No1) 2017-2018* (Cth).[133] The Court addressed this issue in two stages: first, to construe the requirements for this precondition and, second, whether they had been, in fact, satisfied in this instance.

In relation to the first stage, the Court observed that to meet the precondition, the Finance Minister must be satisfied that there is a need for expenditure in the current fiscal year not otherwise provided for, or insufficiently provided for,[134] and that such expenditure is urgent.[135] The Minister's view must be formed reasonably and on a correct understanding of the law,[136] but there exists no obligation to act 'apolitically or quasi-judicially'.[137] The Court rejected the submission that although a voluntary postal vote may not have been foreseen by the executive, expenditure 'directed to achieving the same or a similar result' to the plebiscite generally might have been foreseen, holding that the relevant question is instead 'was *that* expenditure

---

130. *Wilkie v The Commonwealth, Australian Marriage Equality Ltd v Cormann* (2017) 349 ALR 1, 21 [87].
131. *Wilkie v The Commonwealth, Australian Marriage Equality Ltd v Cormann* (2017) 349 ALR 1, 21 [88].
132. *Wilkie v The Commonwealth, Australian Marriage Equality Ltd v Cormann* (2017) 349 ALR 1, 21 [89].
133. *Wilkie v The Commonwealth, Australian Marriage Equality Ltd v Cormann* (2017) 349 ALR 1, 23 [96].
134. *Wilkie v The Commonwealth, Australian Marriage Equality Ltd v Cormann* (2017) 349 ALR 1, 26 [111].
135. *Wilkie v The Commonwealth, Australian Marriage Equality Ltd v Cormann* (2017) 349 ALR 1, 26 [113].
136. *Wilkie v The Commonwealth, Australian Marriage Equality Ltd v Cormann* (2017) 349 ALR 1, 26 [109].
137. *Wilkie v The Commonwealth, Australian Marriage Equality Ltd v Cormann* (2017) 349 ALR 1, 25 [108]–[109].

unforeseen by the Executive Government?'[138] The Court rejected the contention that the Minister erred in law by conflating the statutory requirements—by stating that the expenditure was 'urgent *because* it was unforeseen'.[139] This, the Court found, treated the Minister's statement as 'reasons for an administrative decision', when it was rather identifying s 10(1) of the *Appropriation Act (No1) 2017- 2018* (Cth) pursuant to which the Minister made the determination.[140] Further, the fact that these criteria had been considered separately in the affidavit dispelled any suggestion of conflation.[141]

In light of the Minister's unchallenged affidavit evidence, the Court found that the Minister had satisfied the requirements for the precondition. In other words, the expenditure was urgent 'because the results of the survey were to be known no later than 15 November 2017' and unforeseen as it was not known to the Executive Government that the ABS would conduct a postal survey on same-sex marriage as at 5 May 2017,[142] the last day practical to so provide in the Budget.[143] Rather, that could only be known as at 7 August 2017.[144] Accordingly, the Court concluded that no error of law occurred in issuing the Determination.[145]

(c). Direction

In light of the voluntary nature of the survey, and the regulatory limits on the information that the ABS can collect,[146] the plaintiffs argued

---

138. *Wilkie v The Commonwealth, Australian Marriage Equality Ltd v Cormann* (2017) 349 ALR 1, 28 [120] (emphasis added).
139. *Wilkie v The Commonwealth, Australian Marriage Equality Ltd v Cormann* (2017) 349 ALR 1, 30 [130]–[138] (emphasis added).
140. *Wilkie v The Commonwealth, Australian Marriage Equality Ltd v Cormann* (2017) 349 ALR 1, 30 [131].
141. *Wilkie v The Commonwealth, Australian Marriage Equality Ltd v Cormann* (2017) 349 ALR 1, 30 [132].
142. *Wilkie v The Commonwealth, Australian Marriage Equality Ltd v Cormann* (2017) 349 ALR 1, 30 [133], 31 [136].
143. *Wilkie v The Commonwealth, Australian Marriage Equality Ltd v Cormann* (2017) 349 ALR 1, 11 [36].
144. *Wilkie v The Commonwealth, Australian Marriage Equality Ltd v Cormann* (2017) 349 ALR 1, 31 [137].
145. *Wilkie v The Commonwealth, Australian Marriage Equality Ltd v Cormann* (2017) 349 ALR 1, 31 [138].
146. See *Census and Statistics Act 1905* (Cth).

that the Direction was invalid. This was on the basis that it was outside the statutory power of both the Treasurer to make the Direction, and the ABS to collect the information. This was on three main bases: (i) the opinion on same-sex marriage was not 'statistical information' within the *Australian Bureau of Statistics Act 1975* (Cth), the *Census and Statistics Act 1905* (Cth);[147] (ii) the information was not 'in relation to' matters prescribed in table in s 13 of the Statistics Regulation; and (iii) the Treasurer did not have power to specify from whom the information was to be collected.[148] None of these bases were accepted as they were unsupported by the statutory language.[149]

More specifically, it was held that the meaning of 'statistical information' in the *Census and Statistics Act 1905* (Cth) did not exclude information about personal opinion or belief.[150] The Court noted that the ABS had collected a wide range of data concerning opinions and beliefs in the administration of the Statistics Act since at least the 1960s.[151] Any dichotomy between a 'vote' or 'plebiscite' as opposed to 'statistical information' was found to be false,[152] and ultimately 'information as to the proportion of persons holding a particular opinion or belief, is and always has been "statistical information".'[153]

The Court found that the *Census and Statistics Act 1905* (Cth) provided no justification for reading 'in relation to' as requiring 'anything more than the existence of a relationship'.[154] Accordingly, because the information to be collected was plainly in relation to 'marriages', 'Law' and 'the social . . . characteristics of the population' listed in s 13 of the

---

147. *Wilkie v The Commonwealth, Australian Marriage Equality Ltd v Cormann* (2017) 349 ALR 1, 32 [140]-[144].
148. *Wilkie v The Commonwealth, Australian Marriage Equality Ltd v Cormann* (2017) 349 ALR 1, 32 [141].
149. *Wilkie v The Commonwealth, Australian Marriage Equality Ltd v Cormann* (2017) 349 ALR 1, 32 [143]-[148].
150. *Wilkie v The Commonwealth, Australian Marriage Equality Ltd v Cormann* (2017) 349 ALR 1, 32 [143].
151. *Wilkie v The Commonwealth, Australian Marriage Equality Ltd v Cormann* (2017) 349 ALR 1, 32 [145].
152. *Wilkie v The Commonwealth, Australian Marriage Equality Ltd v Cormann* (2017) 349 ALR 1, 32 [142].
153. *Wilkie v The Commonwealth, Australian Marriage Equality Ltd v Cormann* (2017) 349 ALR 1, 33 [146].
154. *Wilkie v The Commonwealth, Australian Marriage Equality Ltd v Cormann* (2017) 349 ALR 1, 33 [147].

Statistics Regulation, the Court rejected this argument.[155] Moreover, the Court held that there was nothing in the subject-matter, scope or purpose of the Treasurer's power of direction[156] to exclude specification of a target population.[157]

(d). Authority of the AEC to Assist

Section 7A of the *Electoral Act* 1918 (Cth) confers power upon the AEC to make 'arrangements for the supply of goods or services'. The plaintiffs asserted that the AEC was not statutorily authorised to assist the ABS to conduct the postal survey pursuant to this section since the relevant 'power' would be impermissibly exercised outside the AEC's functions.[158] The Court gave short shrift to this argument: because 'arrangements' pursuant to s 7A of the *Electoral Act* 1918 (Cth) constitute one of the AEC's functions, the Court held this was a valid exercise of statutory power.[159]

The rejection of the challenges to the postal survey by the judicial branch of the Commonwealth government cleared the path for the postal survey to proceed between 12 September 2017 and 7 November 2017. On 15 November 2017, the ABS announced the results: of the 79.5% of eligible Australians who responded,[160] an 'overwhelming' 61.6% voted 'yes' 'should the law be changed to allow same-sex couples to marry?'.[161] Acting on the basis of the survey result, the

---

155. *Wilkie v The Commonwealth, Australian Marriage Equality Ltd v Cormann* (2017) 349 ALR 1, 33 [147].
156. *Census and Statistics Act 1905* (Cth) s 9(1)(b).
157. *Wilkie v The Commonwealth, Australian Marriage Equality Ltd v Cormann* (2017) 349 ALR 1, 33 [147].
158. *Wilkie v The Commonwealth, Australian Marriage Equality Ltd v Cormann* (2017) 349 ALR 133 [149].
159. *Wilkie v The Commonwealth, Australian Marriage Equality Ltd v Cormann* (2017) 349 ALR 133 [150].
160. Of the eligible voting population, 12.6 million Australians submitted a clear response, 36,686 submitted a response that was not clear, and 3.2 million did not respond: Australian Bureau Statistics, *National Results* (11 December 2017) Australian Bureau Statistics <http://www.abs.gov.au/ausstats/abs@.nsf/Lookup/by%20Subject/1800.0~2017~Main%20Features~Results~8>.
161. Australian Bureau Statistics, *National Results* (11 December 2017) Australian Bureau Statistics <http://www.abs.gov.au/ausstats/abs@.nsf/Lookup/by%20Subject/1800.0~2017~Main%20Features~Results~8>.

Commonwealth enacted the *Marriage Amendment (Definition and Religious Freedoms) Act 2017* (Cth). We turn now to that final stage of the Australian journey to marriage equality.

B. *Marriage Amendment (Definition and Religious Freedoms) Act 2017* (Cth)

Shortly after the ABS announced the results of the postal survey, the Prime Minister announced that the *Marriage Act 1961* (Cth) would be amended before Christmas so as to provide for same-sex marriage, stating that '[t]he Australian people have spoken in their millions and they have voted overwhelmingly "yes" for marriage equality. Now it is our job to deliver it'.[162] And later that same day, Senator Dean Smith introduced the Marriage Amendment (Definition and Religious Freedoms) Bill 2017 (Cth) in the Senate.[163]

The Bill passed the Senate on 29 November 2017,[164] and the House of Representatives without amendment on 8 December 2017.[165] Having received Royal Assent on 9 December 2017, the Bill entered into force as the *Marriage Amendment (Definition and Religious Freedoms) Act 2017* (Cth) (*MAA*).[166] This achieved, a little more than three weeks after the announcement of the results of the postal sur-

---

162. Joe Kelly and Greg Brown 'Same-sex marriage vote result live: Yes vote wins, Brandis brokers deal with conservatives' *The Australian* (online), 15 November 2017 <https://sslcam.news.com.au/cam/authorise?channel=pc&url=http%3a%2f%2fwww.theaustralian.com.au%2fnational-affairs%2fsamesex-marriage-result-live-vote-details-news-opinion%2fnews-story%2f453863f06bad272ad58b9c8c8d4a8f88>.
163. ABC News, 'Same-Sex Marriage Bill', *ABC News* (online), 16 November 2017 <http://www.abc.net.au/news/2017-11-16/full-text-dean-smith-same-sex-marriage-bill-speech/9157270>.
164. Parliament of Australia, *Marriage Amendment (Definition and Religious Freedoms) Bill 2017* (December 2017) Parliament of Australia <https://www.aph.gov.au/Parliamentary_Business/Bills_Legislation/Bills_Search_Results/Result?bId=s1099>.
165. Parliament of Australia, *Marriage Amendment (Definition and Religious Freedoms) Bill 2017* (December 2017) Parliament of Australia <https://www.aph.gov.au/Parliamentary_Business/Bills_Legislation/Bills_Search_Results/Result?bId=s1099>.
166. <https://www.aph.gov.au/Parliamentary_Business/Bills_Legislation/Bills_Search_Results/Result?bId=s1099>.

vey, the legalisation of same-sex marriage in Australia, permitting couples to lodge a Notice of Intended Marriage to commence the notice period required precedent to marriage under the *Marriage Act 1961* (Cth).[167]

This section examines the principal provisions of the legislation, which fall into two broad categories: those which amend the *Marriage Act 1961* (Cth) so as to provide for same-sex marriage and those which provide for the protection of the interests of those who oppose same-sex marriage on religious grounds.

Providing for Same-Sex Marriage

The keystone of the *MAA* was to provide marriage equality by providing for the solemnisation of marriages for same-sex couples and through the recognition of such marriages solemnised elsewhere.[168] In respect of the former, prior to its amendment by the *MAA*, s 5(1) of the *Marriage Act 1961* (Cth) defined marriage as 'the union of a man and a woman to the exclusion of all others, voluntarily entered into for life'. Using a definition similar to that found in the Canadian *Civil Marriage Act*,[169] the *MAA* replaces this definition with the gender-neutral 'the union of two people, to the exclusion of all others, voluntarily entered into for life', thereby providing equal access to marriage for same-sex couples.[170]

In respect of marriages solemnised in foreign countries, s 88EA of the *Marriage Act 1961* (Cth) had prohibited the recognition of such same-sex marriages. The *MAA* repealed this provision so as to provide for the recognition of such marriages that have been or will be solemnised in under the law of a foreign country as valid in Australia.[171] As such, same-sex couples who were previously married overseas, in foreign consulates on Australian soil, or in the ACT during

---

167. Jessica Haynes, 'When Can Same-Sex Couples Lodge Their Notice for Intended Marriage Forms?' *ABC News* (online), 8 December 2017 <http://www.abc.net.au/news/2017-12-07/when-can-you-lodge-your-notice-for-intended-marriage-forms/9238438>.
168. *Marriage Amendment (Definition and Religious Freedoms) Act 2017* sch 1 pt 1 s 2A.
169. *Civil Marriage Act*, SC 2005, c C-33.
170. *Marriage Amendment (Definition and Religious Freedoms) Act 2017* sch 1 pt 1 s 2A(c).
171. *Marriage Amendment (Definition and Religious Freedoms) Act 2017* sch 1 pt 1 s 71.

the period before the *Marriage Equality (Same Sex) Act 2013* (ACT) was struck down by the High Court will have their marriages automatically and retrospectively recognised.

Protecting Freedom of Religious Belief and Practice

Australia fails to provide for the protection of religious belief and practice in relation to laws that have as their effect, as opposed to their express purpose, the infringement of religious belief and practice.[172] As such, the interests of those who might oppose same-sex marriage on religious grounds required some protection in the *MAA* itself. Those interests fall into two broad areas: those of ministers of religion, religious marriage celebrants or chaplains to refuse to solemnise a same-sex marriage, and those of bodies established for religious purposes who might refuse to provide facilities, goods and services to same-sex couples for a marriage.

In order to protect religious freedom and to respect the 'doctrines, tenets and beliefs' of ministers and the views of their religious community,[173] s 47 of the *MAA* permits a minister of religion to refuse to solemnise a marriage[174] where such refusal conforms to their own religious beliefs, the beliefs or doctrines of their religion, or where it is necessary to avoid damaging the 'religious susceptibilities' of adherents of that religion.[175] Section 47A affords the same right to refuse to religious marriage celebrants if their religious beliefs do not allow them to do so.[176] Notably, these marriage celebrants are required to advertise themselves as a 'religious marriage celebrant' to ensure that couples wanting to marry will know that they may refuse to

---

172. See Paul Babie and Neville Rochow, 'Feels Like Déjà vu: Religious Freedom under a Proposed Australian Bill of Rights' (2010) *BYU Law Review* 821; Paul Babie, 'National Security and the Free Exercise Guarantee of Section 116: Time for a Judicial Interpretive Update', in *Federal Law Review*, 45 (2017): 351.
173. *Marriage Amendment (Definition and Religious Freedoms) Act 2017* sch 1 s 2A(c).
174. *Marriage Amendment (Definition and Religious Freedoms) Act 2017* sch 1 s 47(3).
175. *Marriage Amendment (Definition and Religious Freedoms) Act 2017* sch 1 s 47(4).
176. *Marriage Amendment (Definition and Religious Freedoms) Act 2017* sch 1 s 47A(1).

solemnise their marriage.[177] Similar protections extend to Australian Defence Force chaplains in relation to members of the ADF who wish to marry while deployed overseas; the *MAA* also introduces 'marriage officers' for the ADF, providing a secular alternative to religious marriage, which cannot be refused on discriminatory grounds.[178]

Civil marriage celebrants, however, cannot decline to marry same-sex couples. Civil marriage celebrants whose registration was current on 8 December 2017 when the Bill received assent were given ninety days to transfer their status to religious marriage celebrants so as to decline to perform same-sex weddings on religious grounds.[179] It was estimated that up to three per cent of marriage celebrants would elect to transfer to become religious marriage celebrants when the Bill commenced.[180]

Under existing anti-discrimination laws, bodies established for religious purposes can refuse to provide facilities, goods and services to LGBTI people and others in line with that organisation's doctrine or the congregation's needs.[181] Section 47B of the *MAA* replicates this existing religious exemption for bodies established for religious purposes, such that they may decline to make facilities, goods and services available for the purposes of a marriage or purposes that are 'reasonably incidental' to this, if the refusal aligns with the religious beliefs of the body.[182] Commercial businesses or individuals, however, cannot refuse to provide facilities, goods and services on religious grounds.

During the final stages of the debate on the bill in the House of Representatives, some members sought to introduce amendments to the *MAA* so as to protect the freedom of speech of those individuals or groups who might oppose same-sex marriage. These amendments

---

177. *Marriage Amendment (Definition and Religious Freedoms) Act 2017* sch 1 s 47A(1).sub-div E.
178. *Marriage Amendment (Definition and Religious Freedoms) Act 2017* sch 1 sch 1 s 71A.
179. *Marriage Amendment (Definition and Religious Freedoms) Act 2017* sch 1 sch 1 s 39DD(2).
180. Human Rights Law Centre, Explainer: Marriage Equality in Australia (14 November 2017) Human Rights Law Centre <https://www.hrlc.org.au/news/2017/11/14/explainer-marriage-equality-in-australia>.
181. See, for example, *Sex Discrimination Act 1984* (Cth) s 37.
182. *Marriage Amendment (Definition and Religious Freedoms) Act 2017* sch 1 s 47B(1).

were ultimately rejected. Instead, a panel chaired by former Immigration Minister Philip Ruddock reviewed the protection of religious freedoms in respect of same-sex marriage, with a final report due to be released in the second half of 2018.[183]

Concluding Reflections

Australia, rarely, in traversing the terrain between balancing the competing interests between equality and religious freedom, charts the shortest distance between two points. Marriage equality is no exception to that general rule. Yet, while it has been a difficult passage over a lengthy period, marriage equality has nonetheless been achieved.

No doubt there will be those left disappointed in both camps. There will be those who would have preferred to see no protections for religious freedom, arguing that this is merely compounding what already amounts to significant historical discrimination.[184] And, there are those who would have preferred to see much stronger religious protections extending to speech and to non-religious individuals and businesses. Still, a balance has been struck, at long last, which legalises marriage equality within a broader context of recognising that no right is absolute, either of equality or of religious freedom. Every right is susceptible of some limitation within a liberal democracy such as that found in Australia's federal system.

---

183. Stephanie Borys, 'Philip Ruddock To Review Religious Protections Amid Same-Sex Marriage Debate', ABC News (online) 22 November 2017 <http://www.abc.net.au/news/2017-11-22/same-sex-marriage-philip-ruddock-to-review-religious-protections/9178558>. And see Commonwealth, *Legal Foundations of Religious Freedom in Australia Interim Report*: Joint Standing Committee on Foreign Affairs, Defence and Trade (2017) 1–3.
184. On this, see Laira Krieg and Paul Babie, 'The Space for Religion in Australian Society: An Assessment of the Impact of Australian Anti-Discrimination Legislation on Religious Freedom' in *Child Sexual Abuse, Society and the Future of the Church*, edited by Hilary Regan (Adelaide: ATF Press, 2013): 83–115.

Action and Motive in Economic and Christian Ethics

Geoffrey Brennan[1] and Chris White[2]

Introduction

This paper is conceived as an aid to communication between economists and (Christian) theologians.

At first sight, this may seem to be a singularly pointless exercise. Economists in general do not believe that theology has anything of significance to teach them. And though theologians may well think that the gospel has implications for economic matters, mostly they do not appear to think that the methods of mainstream economics are likely to be helpful in uncovering what those implications are. So 'aiding communication' looks like supplying something for which there is next to no demand. The economists assure us that this is generally a bad idea!

As might be expected from our writing this paper, we ourselves believe that both sides do have something to gain from understanding the other, but we concede at the outset that that is not a commonly shared view.

---

1. Professor Geoffrey Brennan is a faculty member in the Philosophy Program within the Research School of Social Sciences at the Australian National University. He is also a professor of philosophy at the University of North Carolina at Chapel Hill, and a professor of political science at Duke University.
2. Dr Chris White is an actuary who spent most of his full-time career at the international consulting firm Towers Perrin (now Willis Towers Watson). Since leaving that firm he has inter alia studied and taught ethics in a variety of contexts, and worked on his PhD on economics and Christian ethics, supervised by Geoffrey Brennan.

In part, the situation is akin to that with inter-disciplinary traffic generally. The 'life of the mind' is structured around disciplines; and professional incentives encourage a disciplinary focus. Your disciplinary peers are, after all, those who will provide professional recognition: they will decide whether to publish your work, to invite you (or not) to conferences in exotic places, and provide you with the scholarly reputation that will ultimately secure (or not secure) positions in theological colleges or universities. Moreover, disciplinary peers are easier to talk to; they share the same basic language and operate on the same conceptual landscape; they have read the same books and tend to share disciplinary heroes; they have an interest in the same kinds of questions. Even those disciplines that are themselves sites of fierce contestation—as some in the social sciences and humanities are—there is at least broad agreement as to where the fault lines lie and usually some common understanding of what the issues at stake are.

As it happens, economics is a pretty peaceable kingdom in this respect: the vast majority share a common method, and a common sense of what a 'proper education' in the subject amounts to, and of whom the heroes of the discipline are. But peace *within* economics has gone with an imperialist disposition *without*. Over the last two or three decades, there has been a minor industry within economics that involves applying more or less standard methods and analytic techniques to issues traditionally associated with sociology, political science, criminology, law and demography. This is not inter-disciplinary work in any ordinary sense. When economists wander into other territory, it is not on the basis that economists might have something to learn from the locals. It is rather with the intention of applying the 'economic way of thinking' to non-traditional subject-matter. The locals usually object to this kind of colonisation—but that reaction does not much worry the colonisers![3]

One area that has not proven attractive to economists as offering scope for potential colonisation is theology. Although there is a literature on the 'economics of religion', it tends to be focused on so-called

---

3. It does though tend to establish the dividing lines between disciplines as fronts in ongoing methodological warfare.

'religious behaviour' (church-going, financial contributions and the like) rather than on theological questions.[4]

On the other side of the disciplinary divide, theologians who wish to write about 'economic issues' have similar professional incentives to conceive those issues in terms that fellow theologians are likely to understand, deploying categories and methods familiar from the home discipline. Theologians have limited incentives to try to understand economic phenomena in the terms that professional economists understand them, to 'get inside the economist's mind' as we might put it. The truth is that inter-disciplinary communication is hard work and it has limited professional pay-off. And one doesn't have to be an economist to suspect that when the intellectual costs of undertaking an activity are high and the professional benefits from it low, there will not be much enthusiasm for pursuing it!

There is however one constituency for whom relations between theology and economics is a matter of considerable interest. This is the subset of professional economists who self-identify as Christians. These people are not usually also professional theologians: they are more 'consumers' than 'producers' in theological circles. But for such people, the exercise of juggling the claims—and specifically the intellectual claims—of their twin 'professions' becomes very significant at a personal level. It is ultimately a question of internal intellectual coherence. And especially for *academic* Christian economists, coming to a satisfactory mind about where and how Christian convictions fit together with the modes of thinking deployed in analysing the socio-economic order, is a serious challenge on which much depends. Failure to engage that task involves either self-deception or intellectual laziness or both: it is to accept, too easily, a radically disintegrated self.

---

4. An exception is the work of Ekelund *et al* on the doctrine of purgatory and the related practice of intercessory prayer. See Robert B Ekelund, Robert F Hébert, Robert D Tollison, Gary M Anderson and Audrey B Davidson, *Sacred Trust: The Medieval Church as an Economic Firm* (New York/Oxford: Oxford University Press, 1996). Observing that this doctrine/practice created a demand for institutions that could reliably contract to pray for the 'souls of the departed', and that this demand had significant consequences for the wealth of the church and for 'contemplative orders', Ekelund *et al* purport to explain those doctrines and practices (their survival if not their creation) in terms of 'economic forces'.

In short, Christian economists have a well-defined interest in promoting conversation between economics and theology—and this group cannot help but be aware of areas where the tensions between the two areas of enquiry are most pressing. For example, economists need for their analysis some conception of human nature. So do theologians. If these conceptions differ (as they seem to), the conflict is one that ideally demands resolution. And such resolution requires a certain amount of prior agreement about the meaning of terms, and the precise questions on which disagreement appears to emerge. As Renford Bambrough in particular has emphasised, genuine disagreement can only take place in the context of a certain amount of prior agreement about more basic matters: there has to be some common ground on which antagonists can lock horns. Otherwise what appears to be disagreement is simply talking at cross-purposes! In that sense, genuine disagreement is an intellectual accomplishment.

One minimal requirement in securing such disagreement is a common understanding about the use of terms. This is especially important in the economics/theology case because lots of terms widely used in economics are effectively terms of art: they have a very particular disciplinary meaning rather different from the meaning these terms take in ordinary discourse. So for example 'scarcity', 'competition', 'cost', 'self-interest', 'preference', 'rationality' are often understood quite differently in economist circles from the way they tend to be interpreted by disciplinary outsiders.

Furthermore, there is value *within* the discipline in achieving this kind of terminological clarity: economists can be vague or confused or sloppy about the use of terms, often unconsciously slipping from professional meanings to folk meanings, or allowing connotations from those folk meanings to do inappropriate interpretative work.

A second important task is to be alert to presumptions that are important in a discipline that are often not articulated. And this brings us to the issue that is central in the present paper. Our object is to underline a contrast between the *normative posture* typically taken in economics and that typical in Christian theology. Of course, it might be claimed that economics is not committed to any kind of normative framework at all—that economics is a science and that the intrusion of any normative element simply serves to undermine its scientific status.[5] In practice, however, economists have never been reluctant to offer 'policy advice'. Whenever economists offer such advice, they bring to bear a normative framework that emphasises behaviour or human *action*. And indeed, this is so embedded as a part of the professional culture that they may find it hard to imagine that normative analysis might plausibly focus on something else.

By contrast, the Christian tradition has focused much more on issues of agent 'virtue'—understood not just in terms of the actions that agents take but also (and irreducibly) in terms of the motives that lie behind those actions. For this reason, major preoccupations of economists in understanding the workings of social institutions may well seem entirely second-order in the Christian scheme; and equally, the kinds of questions that theology wishes to pose in relation to social institutions will strike the economist as largely beside the point. We shall seek to illustrate this claim by reference to the evaluation of the market and more broadly to 'invisible hand' mechanisms of the kind important in economics since the time of Adam Smith.

We shall approach the central contrast that we seek to underline here by drawing the basic distinction, and in the interests of clarity contrasting our central distinction with the consequentialism/ deontology distinction with which it might be confused. We then provide a more extensive account of the Christian motive-oriented approach, followed by our illustration of the rival economist/ Christian approaches by an examination of the idea of 'invisible hand mechanisms' from each perspective. Finally, we offer a brief conclusion.

The Basic Distinction

The distinction drawn here involves a difference in the respective normative positions adopted in economics and in the Christian tradi-

---

5. Christian theology, commonly described in St Anselm's phrase as 'faith seeking understanding', does not claim scientific status in this sense. Rather than seeking the arguably impossible goal of a disinterested, empirically-based understanding of God, Christian theology can be described as an active love seeking a deeper knowledge of the divine mystery of the triune God. For a discussion of the task of theology, see Daniel L Migliore, *Faith Seeking Understanding: An Introduction to Christian Theology* (Grand Rapids: Eerdmans, 1991) 1–18.

tion. After discussing this difference in some detail, we comment on the respective economic and Christian positions on the significance of the 'invisible hand' tradition—the idea that pursuit of self-interest[6] produces outcomes which are socially beneficial overall—before touching briefly on differences between the two disciplines on the social role of markets.

As a religious faith, Christianity takes a normative position, the understanding of which is the subject of Christian theology and ethics. There is, of course, frequently considerable contention among Christian theologians and ethicists (collectively referred to in this paper as 'Christians') about the *content* of that normative position, but the basic issue under consideration, the fundamental normativity of the faith, is uncontentious.

However, the issue is contentious for economics, because many economists deny that the discipline is committed to a normative position. On that view, economics is a science—an essentially descriptive/explanatory enterprise, which in principle involve no value judgments at all, as represented in a famous statement by Lionel Robbins: 'ethical value judgments have no place in scientific analysis.'[7] Perhaps ethical requirements can be added to the system of explanation to provide 'policy advice' or a normatively-based defence of certain social institutions. But any such ethical component is seen as superfluous to economics as a scientific discipline: on this view it is an add-on without any credentials within the economics discipline as such.

Even if this view of economics were accepted, there is an identifiable focus of explanation which attaches most naturally to certain kinds of ethical evaluation (and not to others). Specifically, econom-

---

6. Self-interest in this context is not necessarily 'selfish', but represent the wider expression of the individual's interests, including concerns for others and the wider array of social concerns which the individual may have.
7. Lionel Robbins, *An Essay on the Nature and Significance of Economic Science* (London: Macmillan, 1932). The statement has been widely quoted and discussed, for example, by Paul Samuelson, who asserts the correctness of Robbins' view. Paul A Samuelson, *Foundations of Economic Analysis* (Harvard: Harvard University Press, 1983/1947), 219f. For a contemporary review of the debate on Robbins's view see Andrea Scarantino, 'On the role of values in economic science: Robbins and his critics' in *Journal of the History of Economic Theory*, 31/4 (2009): 449–473.

ics concerns itself with human behaviour (in its Austrian tradition, human action)—or more accurately, with changes in that behaviour/action. And this means that normative/ethical systems that focus on action connect with economics in a manner that other normative/ethical systems do not.

In any event, as a purely empirical matter, economists as a profession—whatever their protestations as to the 'scientific' credentials of their findings—have never been reluctant to offer advice on what public policies ought to be followed, or on what institutional arrangements are 'best'. And even if that advice is understood hypothetically—for example, 'if you want to achieve X, do Y'—there is still the presumption that X is what sensible policy makers will or ought to want to do and/or what sensible voters will or ought to vote for.

Clearly, any ethical system involves a specification of the scope of ethical evaluation—that is, defining what it is that matters from an ethical point of view. Within economics, the answer given to that question has been human behaviour/action—and the social outcomes to which that behaviour/action gives rise. Within the Christian tradition by contrast, there has been much more attention to the issue of agent motive: inclination or disposition or attitude or intention or will. And it is this action/motive distinction which is the object of focus here.

The thought that the distinction between the economist and the Christian tracks the distinction between outcome-focus and motive-focus might not be so obvious if one focuses simply on the writings of Christians on public policy questions. Often such writings proceed by treating the Christian position as if it had direct implications for substantive policy. Thus, declarations by Christians on issues such as abortion, or euthanasia, or sweatshops in developing countries, or the environment, do not obviously focus on the motives of the relevant agents: those declarations usually deal primarily with agents' actions, or the legal and public policy issues to which those actions give rise. The difference between economists and Christians in terms of our 'basic distinction' we see as one of emphasis. It is true that the great majority of economists are inclined to think that action is all that counts, but we do not think that Christians are committed to a focus on motive to the same extent. Just where the weight between motive and action in the Christian tradition properly lies is doubtless a matter of some argument. Nevertheless, we think that there is a demonstrable difference between economists and Christians on this matter, and that this difference is something that needs to be borne in mind in communication across this 'disciplinary divide'.

Further, the Christian tradition has no monopoly on a concern with agent motivation. The Kantian tradition for example deprecates any action that is not driven by a sense of duty towards the requirements of the moral law—no act can have moral worth that is not driven by the intention to fulfil the moral law's requirements. Similarly, virtue ethics (of the kind advanced by Plato and Aristotle, *inter alia*[8]) identifies the character of the actor rather than the action performed as the central ethical concern. In this case, motive and mode of deliberation and the nature of the agent's inclinations all figure—over and above the actions undertaken. But it does seem that a central element in specifically Christian ethics is that motives matter—that it is not enough to be obedient to the letter of the law, as the scribes and Pharisees were. The law must be inscribed on the heart—that it is possible to sin by 'thought' as well as by 'word' and 'deed'.[9] Having bad thoughts (lust for another's wife, or anger towards one's brother) is, in the words of Jesus, a type of sin (Mt 5:21–30).

The Pauline triad of faith, hope and love (1 Cor 13:13) all invoke an indispensable attitudinal dimension. Paul makes it clear that love, the superior of these qualities of Christian ethical character, does not reduce to actions—'If I give all I possess to the poor and surrender my body to the flames, but have not love, I gain nothing' (1 Cor 13:3).[10]

The conceptual landscape relevant to the discussion that follows thus has three elements: actions, motives, and the relation between them. And our aim is to contrast economics and Christian theology in relation to those elements. Accordingly, the argument can be usefully presented in terms of the following matrix (Figure 1).

---

8. Contemporarily including Alasdair MacIntyre, *After Virtue: A Study in Moral Theory*, second edition (London: Duckworth, 1985).
9. Word as well as deed can be treated as a kind of action. The decision to articulate a thought, perhaps unlike the thought itself, is a matter over which the agent can be thought to exercise greater control.
10. For discussion of the textual difficulties of this verse, see Gordon D Fee, *The First Epistle to the Corinthians*, The New International Commentary on the New Testament (Grand Rapids: Eerdmans, 1987), 629.

Figure 1 Action/Motive Distinction Between Economics and Christianity

	Action	Motive	Connection
Christian	derivative	predominant	conceptually complex
Economics	predominant	derivative	conceptually direct

Simply put, economics and the Christian tradition differ in what they focus on in terms of normative evaluation—and hence what requires to be explained and analysed. Economics focuses on action: motive has a derivative role, relevant only insofar as it influences action. But the connection between motive and action is conceptually direct: for the great majority of economists, agents are uniformly taken to be basically rational in the Humean sense.[11] The Christian tradition focuses on motive; action has a second-order role as a signal of motive, but the relation between motive and action is conceptually complex and arguably a matter of contestation between various sources (the features of which are explored below).

Consequentialism vs Deontology

It will serve to clarify the conceptual framework set out in the previous section to differentiate our distinction from the consequentialism/deontology distinction with which it is sometimes confused. There are a number of ways in which deontology and consequentialism can be distinguished, but as we see it there are three important dimensions in terms of which differences and also complexities emerge:

1. One dimension relates to the position taken towards the scope of ethical evaluation specifically, whether the actor is called on to act so as to maximise/optimise the achievement of the specified value, or to act so as to instantiate or exemplify that value. Suppose for example the ethical system specifies truth-telling as the normatively relevant consideration. The consequentialist then thinks that each should act to secure the maximal amount of truth-telling overall. In particular, if by my telling a lie, I can bring about

---

[11]. Behavioural economists, while exploring the implications of evidence counter to this neoclassical assumption of rationality, are still primarily interested in how agents' psychological dispositions influence their actions.

greater truth-telling overall, I should tell the lie.[12] The deontologist thinks that I should not—that my obligation is to uphold the relevant value of truth-telling by exemplifying that value in my own conduct. This difference is often described by reference to a tension between doing what is 'right' (deontology) and doing what is 'good' (consequentialism). It can be captured by a more precise definition of the ethical value—either the truth-telling specifically of the individual agent, or truth-telling in general.

2. Secondly, there are complexities in choosing between the 'right' and the 'good' in many situations, independently of whether actions or motives are predominant in our ethical framework. In many such situations, we may reasonably argue that adopting a deontological position to the exclusion of a consequentialist one (or *vice versa*) results in untenable outcomes at extremes, despite that in our 'redeemed' moments we may even perceive both positions as identical.[13] Thus, an economist may be *predominantly* a consequentialist, but agree that there are some circumstances in which a deontological position or element needs to be factored in. Conversely, a Christian may be *predominantly* a deontologist, but accept that on occasion there may be a need to have some regard for consequences. For example, an overlap between 'right' and 'good' can emerge when the predominant consequentialist argues 'what but the ends can justify the means?'—surely, only some ends justify some means, and not that any ends justify any

---

12. The possibility is not totally fanciful. Suppose I do not believe in eternal damnation, but know that if I promote the view that lying leads to eternal damnation, that will increase truth-telling. Or suppose that I happen upon evidence that lying is much more common than people generally believe it to be. I realise that, were this evidence to become common knowledge, standards will fall and people will be less inhibited about lying (for esteem-related reasons: see Geoffrey Brennan and Philip Pettit, *The Economy of Esteem: An Essay on Civil and Political Society* (Oxford: Oxford University Press, 2004)). I am asked in a public forum how common lying is. If I lie and say 'rare', that may well have the effect of reducing lying overall. In each case, a consequentialist will tell the lie, whereas a deontologist will not.

13. 'In moments of grace we may be given the perception that our duty and our fulfilment are one and the same, and we may speak of that unity in hope and faith; but we cannot ask that we should never be challenged to further thought and conscientious struggle by an awareness of the divergence of inclination and duty.' Oliver O'Donovan, *Resurrection and Moral Order: An Outline for Evangelical Ethics*, second edition (Grand Rapids: Eerdmans, 1994), 139.

means. The predominant deontologist might reject this proposition, asking 'shall we do evil that good may come?' but all save the most extreme deontologists would be prepared to argue that 'let right be done though the heavens fall' is more immoral. Only a few of those who are predominant deontologists would argue that a lie is never justified (such as to save an innocent life), or that the violence in pushing someone out of the path of the proverbial runaway truck is in the same category as the same level of violence with the objective of injury. The point is that the means and ends must be 'fitting',[14] whether stemming from action or motive or a mixture of both, and hence this complexity in the application of consequentialist and deontological methodologies has a distinguishable character from action and motive.[15]

3. A third (and independent) feature of the difference relates to the metric of evaluation. Deontologists tend to talk in terms of 'permissibility/ impermissibility'—so in relation to truth-telling, there is a simple binary relation between action and rightness.[16] Consequentialists tend to talk in terms of degrees: when I tell a lie to increase truth-telling by others, there is a calculation required as to whether aggregate truth-telling goes up (recognising that my lying serves to reduce truth-telling in aggregate). However, in that consequentialist calculation there is no necessary presumption that each instance of lying is equally bad. Specific instances of lying can be evaluated, for example, by assessing how great is the difference between what is said and what is true. Often, of course, lying is itself a means to a further end—or even if valued intrinsically, is not the only intrinsically valued object under consideration. So it may be that a 'white lie' is measured not so much by

---

14. This 'mixed' ethical approach, combining the good, the right and the fitting (or the teleological, the deontological and the ethological) is that recommended by Max Stackhouse in resolving complex ethical situations - see his introductory essay in *On Moral Business: Classical and Contemporary Resources for Ethics in Economic Life*, edited by Max L Stackhouse, Dennis P McCann, Shirley J Roels and Preston N Williams (Grand Rapids: Eerdmans, 1995), 31.
15. For a more extensive discussion see James A Whyte 'Ends and Means', in *A New Dictionary of Christian Ethics*, edited by John Macquarrie and James Childress (London: SCM Press, 1967): 191f.
16. The categories can produce a three-valued metric, since not-performing X may be impermissible (that is performing X may be obligatory)—so performing X may be impermissible, permissible or obligatory.

reference to how far from the truth it sits, but rather by what the assessed effect of the lie is on the well-being of the person lied to. As already pointed out, this 'metric' aspect operates independently of the ethical scope. So a deontologist might work with a two- or three-valued metric, whereas a consequentialist might measure the 'ethical performance' by means of a continuous value-metric (which is individual and not meaningfully comparable with the corresponding metrics of others).

The important point for our purpose, however, is that however precisely the characteristics of the deontology/consequentialism distinction are drawn, that distinction is not the same as the distinction between motive and action. In the matrix shown in Figure 2, all the illustrative entries are possible: one might be an action deontologist or a motive deontologist; and though consequentialist theories are usually applied to actions, there is nothing to preclude the possibility that the consequentialist end to be maximized is a particular motive or attitude.[17]

Figure 2 Specimen Differences of Deontology/Consequentialism and Action/Motive

	Deontology	**Consequentialism**
Action	Pharisees in relation to the 'law'	Standard utilitarianism
Motive	Kantian internalisation of moral law	Maximisation of 'love'

Figure 2 sets out relatively uncontroversial and familiar examples of each category, though in some ways, each of the entries is somewhat question-begging. For example, some elements of the law mandate attitudes (for example, the covetousness of the tenth commandment of the Hebrew Bible); and it is arguable whether 'love' can be understood in terms of motive alone independent of consequent action. Nevertheless, the cases seem sufficient to establish that the action/motive distinction and the deontology/consequentialism distinction are different distinctions. It is therefore appropriate to set the latter distinction aside for our present purpose.

---

17. See, for example, Robert M Adams, 'Motive Utilitarianism' in *Journal of Philosophy*, 73 (1976): 467–481.

Christian Perspectives on Actions and Motives

For the Christian, the defining commandment is arguably that set out in Jesus' answer to the testing question of a Pharisee lawyer: 'Teacher, which commandment in the law is the greatest?' to which Jesus replies:

> 'You shall love the Lord your God with all your heart, and with all your soul, and with all your mind.' This is the greatest and first commandment. And a second is like it: 'You shall love your neighbour as yourself.' On these two commandments hang all the law and the prophets (Mt 22:36–40).

Mark (12:28-31) also records this interchange, and, significantly, adds 'and with all your strength' to the list in the first commandment,[18] possibly suggesting that the commandment extends beyond motive ('heart', 'soul', and 'mind') to action ('strength').

This emphasis in, and the all-encompassing scope of, Jesus' first, pre-eminent commandment reflect the fundamental connection of his teaching to Jewish theology. He is quoting the *Shema Yisrael*, the first and great commandment of the Ten Commandments (Dt 6:4), the most important part of the Jewish prayer service, and recited twice daily by observant Jews. The source of the second and equal commandment of Jesus is found in the law: 'You shall not take vengeance or bear a grudge against any of your people, but you shall love your neighbour as yourself' (Lev 19:18), probably the earliest statement of what has become known as the Golden Rule. However, Jesus radically extends its application beyond the household of Israel to all people, notably in his definition of 'neighbour' in the parable of the Good Samaritan.[19]

The primary requirement of 'love' in these overall statements of the moral law of both the Hebrew Bible and the New Testament drives us from the field of moral action to the moral subject, from this or that act which the subject might perform, from the question of whether it is a good or a bad act and the extent to which it does or does not result from love, to the subject him or herself, whether he or she is a good

---

18. So also Luke (10:25–28), who shows Jesus using the first commandment in the prelude to the parable of the Good Samaritan.
19. See previous footnote. The Samaritans were roundly disliked, even hated, by the Jews, and the two groups normally had nothing to do with each other (See Jn 4:9).

or a bad person, and to what extent he or she is motivated by love. As well as exploring what love means in this context, we also look at the New Testament concept of what actions stem from love, what motivates love, particularly at the meaning of the related New Testament concept of 'heart', and how those actions and motivations interact.

Not all commentators agree that 'love' is the defining characteristic of Christian ethics. Hays, in a very influential book,[20] sets out three tests for what he calls the 'focal images' of New Testament ethics, which ask of the candidate:

- The extent to which it finds a textual basis in all of the canonical witnesses;
- If it stands in serious tension with the ethical teachings or major emphases of any of the New Testament witnesses;
- If it highlights central and substantial ethical concerns of the texts in which it appears.[21]

By a thorough application of these tests to the New Testament canon, Hays derives three focal images of New Testament ethics—community, cross and new creation.[22] He deals with the objection that he has erroneously omitted love by arguing:

- that love is not a focal image in (at least) Mark, Acts, Hebrews and Revelation,
- that rather than a focal image, love is more properly an interpretation of an image, and is embodied concretely in the cross, and
- that the term has become so debased in popular discourse that it has become a cover for what is an assertion of ethical relativism—the 'loving' thing to do is to accept everyone and avoid the difficult demands of the gospel.[23]

Hays's approach is based on the ideal of a unity of focal images throughout the whole of the New Testament canon, rather than accepting some diversity in the emphases of the various texts according to their differing authors, circumstances and settings (which extent of diversity arguably gives the various texts an enhanced authenticity).

---

20. Richard B Hays, *The Moral Vision of the New Testament: A Contemporary Introduction to New Testament Ethics* (New York: HarperCollins, 1996).
21. Hays, *The Moral Vision of the New Testament*, 195.
22. Hays, *The Moral Vision of the New Testament*, 196–200.
23. Hays, *The Moral Vision of the New Testament*, 200–203.

In emphasising the particular words of Jesus from which we have derived love as a focal image, we are of course concentrating on his primary ministry to Jewish people.[24] Hence, our focus is on Jesus' ministry, primarily to Jews and before the Easter event, and so it is not surprising that the cross does not figure in the way that it does in the letters to the early churches, which increasingly included Gentiles.

The three images Hays chooses are excellent foci in the light of the issues and interests of the early church. However, we disagree with him when he says that '[t]he content of the word 'love' is given fully and exclusively in the death of Jesus on the cross; apart from this specific narrative image, the term has no meaning',[25] and hence that love should not be added to the list. Granted, when John records Jesus telling his followers to 'love one another as I have loved you' (Jn 15:12), there would clearly have been the ultimate ethical challenge of Jesus' supreme sacrifice in the minds of John's readers/ listeners. However, the death on the cross of the incarnate Christ, the sinless son of God atoning for their sins and those of the whole world, clearly represented infinitely more by way of love for others than any of his followers could ever imagine emulating. Hence, love as an ethical focus for the post-Easter believer has a meaning related to but subsidiary to Jesus' love for all of humanity in his death on the cross.

Several commentators agree that love is the primary focus of Christian ethics.[26] Richard Burridge, as well as adopting love as the epitome of Jesus' two great commandments and hence as the basis of Christian ethics,[27] deals specifically with Hays's objections. He critiques at some length Hays's complete neglect of the central role played by love in the Pauline letters, particularly its very practical ethical consequences in them.[28] In addition to love's primary place in

---

24. And hence with the strong connections to the ethical basis of the Hebrew Bible; though as pointed out below, in the context of Burridge's analysis, love is also an important theme in the Pauline letters to the early church.
25. Hays, *The Moral Vision of the New Testament*, 202.
26. For example: Wolfgang Schrage *The Ethics of the New Testament*, translated by David E Green (Minneapolis: Fortress Press, 1988), 212f, 216f; Victor P Furnish, *The Love Command in the New Testament* (Nashville: Abingdon Press, 1972), 95; Douglas A Campbell, *The Quest for Paul's Gospel: A Suggested Strategy* (London: T & T Clark, 2005), 117; cited by Richard A Burridge, *Imitating Jesus: An Inclusive Approach to New Testament Ethics* (Grand Rapids: Eerdmans, 2007), 108.
27. Burridge, *Imitating Jesus*, 50–55.
28. Burridge, *Imitating Jesus*, 108–110.

Jesus' two great commandments, he analyses in detail the relationship between love, law and freedom. Summarising an extended and at times complex discussion, Burridge concludes that God's love, what he has done in Christ, is the 'fulfilment of the law' (Gal 5:14, Rom 13:10); it frees the Christian from the law to live a life exemplified in the life and teaching of Jesus in the power of the Holy Spirit.[29]

In addition to Jesus' focus on love, the gospels include many instances of where Jesus rails at the casuistry of the scribes and Pharisees, at their narrowly legalistic application of the law, rather than its spirit. In his primary ethical teaching in the Sermon on the Mount, Jesus both affirms the rules of the Hebrew Bible ('the law [and] the prophets' Mt 5:17–20), and, as just noted, goes beyond ['fulfils'] them, to the motivations, which to many exegetes he appears to equate with the action itself. Thus lusting after a woman is equivalent to committing adultery with her in the heart (Mt 5:27, 28). Christian theology, primarily based in the atoning death of Jesus Christ on the cross, holds that God gives redemption by grace to those who believe and accept his forgiveness for their sins, and even though in their actions they continue to fall short, they can continue to be forgiven after genuine repentance, provided their motivation 'in the heart' is true.

Two biblical characters who are recorded as greatly used by God in the course of salvation history but who are nevertheless fallible, demonstrate the truth of this statement of God's grace towards sinners who genuinely seek forgiveness and maintain a pure heart:

- **David**, whom Samuel pronounces as Saul's successor as King of Israel because he is 'a man after God's own heart' (1 Sam 13:14). This is despite David's subsequent adultery with Bathsheba and deliberate murder of her husband Uriah (2 Sam 11). But when confronted over his sin by Nathan the prophet and punished by the death of his and Bathsheba's child, David admits his sin and seeks God's forgiveness (2 Sam 12:3–20, and Ps 51). David continues to be God's anointed king of both Israel and Judah in the Hebrew Bible (for example Ezek 37:24f), from whose line the Messiah will come (for example Isa 9:7), and is confirmed as 'a man after God's own heart' in the New Testament by Paul at Pisidian Antioch (Acts 13:22).

---

29. Burridge, *Imitating Jesus*, 110–115.

- **Peter** is called by Jesus as one of the first disciples (Mt 4:18–20), the first disciple to whom God reveals that Jesus is the Messiah (Mt 16:13–17), one of the three disciples with Jesus on the mount of transfiguration (Mt 17:1–13), and declared by Jesus to be the foundation of the church (Mt 16:18–19). Nevertheless he denies Jesus three times after his arrest (Mt 26:69–75), but repents (v 75) and is forgiven. Peter is commissioned by the resurrected Christ to shepherd his flock (Jn 21:15–19), and goes on to be one of the key apostles of the early church. He declares the gospel in Jerusalem to Jews (Acts 2:14–42, Acts 3:11–26, Acts 4:5–22, Acts 5:17–32), and beyond to Gentiles as well (Acts 9:32–10:48), for whom he is instrumental in their acceptance as Christians (Acts 11:1-18).

For our question, then, the significance of action and motive in Christian ethics, Jesus' pre-eminent commandments (recorded in his reply to the Pharisee in Mt 22:36–40), and his development of that statement in his other fundamental ethical teaching, particularly the Sermon on the Mount, requires considerable unpacking.

First, what the New Testament gospel and (particularly) letter writers meant by the word translated as 'love' is a matter on which Biblical scholars have expended considerable energy. Its importance, particularly in Paul's writings, including the seminal verse in 1 Corinthians 13:13: 'And now faith, hope, and love abide; these three, and the greatest of these is love', is reason enough.

There are four words in Greek translated 'love' in English—*storgē* (affection, especially within families) and *eros* (including love between the sexes including erotic love), neither of which are really used in the New Testament, *philia* (friendship, 'brotherly love'), and *agapē* (charity, or self-giving love). Despite being the most widely used word in contemporary Greek literature for 'love', *philia* and its cognates are used very sparingly in the New Testament (mostly in John's gospel). *Agapē* is used rarely in classical Greek, but is the preferred word for love of the New Testament writers (over 100 times), arguably primarily to avoid the associations and/or limitations of the commonly used Greek words of the first century. It is also used widely in the Septuagint (the Greek translation of the Hebrew Bible widely in use at the time of Christ), probably for similar reasons.

Grenz summarises well the arguments for the New Testament and early church writers' use of *agapē*:

> This previously obscure word of uncertain etymology, lacking both the power or magic of *eros* and the warmth of *philia*, was just what the early Christians needed to articulate their understanding of love.
>
> In part the reason for the choice of *agapē* lay in the meaning of the term itself. In classical Greek, the verb form *agapaō* can carry the idea of 'to prefer', 'to set one good or aim above another', 'to esteem one person more highly than another'. As a result it could denote God's preference for a particular person and hence the one whom God blesses with particular gifts and possessions. Consequently to the ancient Greek mind *agapē* spoke of a love that moved beyond emotion—beyond an experience which, in the words of Barclay, 'comes to us unsought, and, in a way, inevitably'. Instead, *agapē* is 'a principle by which we deliberately live'. This kind of love has to do with the mind and the will.[30]

So this love of God and neighbour which is at the core of the Christian life is a self-giving love based in the heart, soul and mind rather than in the emotions. It is the enabler of actions, and, without minimising the importance of actions, transcends them. But, how do Jesus and the synoptic gospel writers understand 'heart', the wellspring of this radical love? One might conclude that, in modern language, it is the motivation for the action which they are emphasising. Some theologians have specifically adopted this position, for example Helmut Thielicke: 'The specifically "Christian" element in ethics is rather to be sought explicitly and exclusively in the motivation of the action.'[31]

Jesus' criticism of the religious leaders of his day was that in spite of their outward conformity to the law, their motives were wrong. They were focused on their own interests, specifically their pride and power, rather than worship of God and care for their people, from which Jesus was able to see they were motivated by selfishness. His divine insight exemplifies the obvious dilemma of motive as a human ethical basis: only the extremely insightful (such as Jesus, and ulti-

---

30. Stanley J Grenz, *The Moral Quest: Foundations of Christian Ethics* (Downers Grove: InterVarsity Press, 1997), 280f.
31. Helmut Thielicke, *Theological Ethics*, translated by John W Doberstein, edited by William H Lazareth, Vol. 1 (Fortress Press, 1966), 20; cited in Grenz, *The Moral Quest*, 229.

mately only God himself) can distinguish good actions done for wrong reasons (or vice versa). Scripture is replete with examples: throughout the Bible, believers are urged to pray, give to the poor, and fast, but Jesus points out that those who do such for selfish reasons will go unrewarded by God. (Mt 6:1–18) And there is a second leg to this dilemma: when a motive (good or bad) never has the opportunity to find fulfilment, this too is opaque to ordinary human eyes. At its most fundamental, the dilemma illustrates the absence of a one-to-one correspondence between a given action and the motive of its agent.[32]

This reason, the difficulty of deducing others' motives from merely observing their actions, lies behind the extensive warnings in the New Testament against judging others (for example Mt 7:1f, Lk 6:37, Rom 14:1–15, Jas 4:12). Meier concludes: 'Since individuals cannot reliably judge others' motives, we have no recourse in human affairs but to 'know a tree by its fruit' (Mt 7:15–20, 12:33, Lk 6:43–45) even while recognizing the limitations of not being able to see another's heart.'[33] In this respect, Christians are of course in the same boat as anyone else, but cannot leave the matter there, recognising the importance of motive (or the 'heart', to use the Biblical writers' majority term), because of God's priority on the innermost wellspring of action.

Even more hazardous is attempting to deduce God's motives based upon his actions; as second Isaiah says:

> For my thoughts are not your thoughts, nor are your ways my ways, says the Lord. For as the heavens are higher than the earth, so are my ways higher than your ways and my thoughts than your thoughts (Isa 55: 8–9).

A New Testament example has Luke recording Jesus as saying to the Pharisees when they scoffed at His teaching that humans cannot serve God and wealth: 'You are those who justify yourselves in the sight of others; but God knows your hearts; for what is prized by human beings is an abomination in the sight of God' (Lk 16:15).

In some cases scripture shows the omniscient God responding to people in respect of their motives (for example 1 Kgs 8:39), in other

---

32. See extended discussion by Samuel A Meier, 'Motives', in Walter A Elwell, editor, *Evangelical Dictionary of Biblical Theology* (Grand Rapids: Baker Books, 1996).
33. Meier, 'Motives'.

cases in respect of their actions (for example Rom 2:2–16), and sometimes with a balance of both (for example Rev 2:23). That our intentions are not always achieved, and frequently that our actions have unintended consequences (both good and bad), make any analysis enormously complex. In any case, how God will judge our motives and actions is doubtless beyond human scrutiny. And God seems to work out his purposes independently of human actions[34] (raising interesting questions about the extent of human free will—an important issue, but beyond our present scope).

Human motives which may never result in action are still subject to divine scrutiny and factored into God's judgment: Jesus equates anger with murder (Mt 5:21,22) and lust with adultery (Mt 5:28).[35] James (4:17) says it is sinful to know the right thing to do, but fail to do it; hence many Christians pray in the liturgy of confession for forgiveness of sins of omission as well as sins of commission. And in the Hebrew Bible, the last of the Ten Commandments prohibits covetousness, independently of any resultant action (unlike the preceding four commandments, which deal specifically with anti-social actions). (Ex 20:17)

Thus, a thought can constitute an act, and is capable of being sinful. However, it seems that it is the deliberate or permissive act of thinking which has the potential for sinfulness, rather than a thought which occurs more or less spontaneously due to some circumstance or stimulus.

The widespread consequentialist view understanding motivation through the resulting impact of an action is in a substantial minority in scripture, as opposed to the majority deontological perspective of the intrinsic value of that action. Assuming a particular outcome is frequently seen in scripture as presumptuous of the future, which cannot be predicted with any certainty; rather one is enjoined to trust God (for example Mt 6:25–34).

---

34. The classic biblical example is in the Genesis record of the life of Joseph (Gen 37–50). In Gen 45:5, after revealing his identity to his brothers, Joseph tells them that 'God sent me before you to preserve life', and when he is eventually reconciled with his brothers after Jacob's death, he tells them 'Even though you intended to do harm to me, God intended it for good, in order to preserve a numerous people . . .'(Gen 50:20).
35. See more extensive discussion below.

Some writers find motivation an inadequate description of what the New Testament states is the ethical core of who human beings are. For example, Grenz says that

> ... even the quest for right motives does not tap the central heartbeat of the New Testament conception of the ethical life. Motivation is itself related to something deeper. According to the New Testament writers the ultimate wellspring of action is our 'heart'...[36]

He goes on to link 'heart' with the virtue of integrity, which in turn he argues leads to uprightness of character, and then, importantly for the Christian, authenticity, courage of conviction, and finally a communitarian virtue ethic.[37]

Or we might turn the definition the other way around, and define virtue in terms of the heart:

> A 'virtue' is a habit of the heart, a stable disposition, a settled state of character, a durable, educated characteristic of someone to exercise her will to be good. The definition would be circular if 'good' meant just the same thing as 'virtuous'. But it's more complicated than that. Alasdair MacIntyre's famous definition is 'A virtue is an acquired human quality the possession of which tends to enable us to achieve those goods which are internal to practices and the lack of which effectively prevents us from achieving such goods.'[38]

Independent of following Grenz or not in this subsequent train of thought, we turn now to the primary word used in the New Testament covering the wellspring of motivations (the 'heart'). When Jesus attacks the scribes and Pharisees for their legalist prioritising of tradition in Mark 7, including the Jewish food laws, he then teaches the disciples that it is what comes from the human heart which is critical:

---

36. Grenz, *The Moral Quest*, 229.
37. Grenz, *The Moral Quest*, 229-239.
38. Deidre N McCloskey, *The Bourgeois Virtues: Ethics for an Age of Commerce* (Chicago: University of Chicago Press, 2006, 64 quoting MacIntyre, *After Virtue*, 178.

> Do you not see that whatever goes into a person from the outside cannot defile, since it enters, not the heart but the stomach . . . It is what comes out of a person that defiles. For it is from within, from the human heart, that evil intentions (*dialogismos* = calculation, reasoning, thought, plotting) come: fornication, theft, murder, adultery, avarice, wickedness, deceit, licentiousness, envy, slander, pride, folly (Mk 7:18b–23).

The word 'heart' (*kardia*) in the New Testament has multiple meanings, the most important of which, according to Behm, are:

(a) the seat of feelings, desires, and passions (for example, joy, pain, love, desire, and lust),
(b) the seat of thought and understanding,
(c) the seat of the will, and
(d) the religious centre to which God turns, which is the root of religious life, and which determines moral conduct.[39]

Behm in this article attributes meaning (b)—the seat of thought and understanding—to the use of *kardia* in this Markan passage.

This judgment is confirmed by the inclusions of *kardia* in the widely recognised Bauer's Greek-English lexicon under the expanded classification as follows:

- the seat of physical, spiritual and mental life
  - as centre and source of the whole inner life, with its thinking, feeling, and volition
    - of the faculty, of the thoughts themselves, of understanding, as the organ of natural and spiritual enlightenment.[40]

O'Donovan questions this interpretation of 'heart' in this Markan passage. He asks:

---

39. J Behm, '*kardia* in the NT,' in Gerhard Kittel & Gerhard Friedrich, editors, translated and abridged in one volume by Geoffrey W Bromiley, *Theological Dictionary of the New Testament* (Grand Rapids: Eerdmans/Paternoster Press, 1985), 416.
40. Walter Bauer, 'καρδία, ας, ἡ' in *A Greek-English Lexicon of the New Testament and Other Early Christian Literature,* second edition translated by W F Arndt and F W Gingrich, further revised and augmented by F W Gingrich and F W Danker (Chicago: University of Chicago Press, 1979/1957), 403.

Could Jesus have meant that every act of foolishness was preceded by a foolish thought? that every act of slander was preceded by a slanderous thought? and that every act of pride was preceded by a proud thought? Did he perhaps mean that none of these acts would be a matter of serious moral concern if they were spontaneous and undeliberated?[41]

His answer is that 'the seat of thought and understanding' is an inadequate interpretation in this context,[42] and that '[t]hese evils arise from the "personal agency" of the one whose acts express them'. He explains:

> They 'defile a man', unlike the food he eats, because they really belong to him. He the moral agent is himself the evil thinker, the fornicator, the thief; he is not merely one who happens to perform fornication, theft or slander, as it were incidentally. The individual is the subject of his own corrupt acts, he is the consummate moral reality which his acts declare. When we are told that God looks upon the heart of a man, this means, not only that God sees certain acts which, by their private character, are hidden from the scrutiny of human observers, but also that he sees and comprehends the subject himself in his totality as a moral being.[43]

Thus, for O'Donovan, Jesus' meaning of 'heart' in this passage goes beyond the 'seat of thoughts and understanding,' to the very core of who we are, in our 'totality as a moral being.' This conception gets to the very core of what Mark's recording of Jesus' use of 'heart' means in this passage. Thoughts and understanding, and, we think, motivations, are a consequence unseen (except by God), rather than who people are in our totality as moral beings.

But O'Donovan does not see the substitution of divine ethical evaluation of the subject him or herself for ethical evaluation of his or her acts; they are correlates, not alternatives. The understanding of this correlation is, in O'Donovan's words, 'the most difficult question that faces an "ethics of character".'[44]

---

41. O'Donovan, *Resurrection and Moral Order*, 205.
42. Though not in other contexts – see below.
43. O'Donovan, *Resurrection and Moral Order*, 205.
44. O'Donovan, *Resurrection and Moral Order*, 205f.

At the risk of over-simplifying his extended discussion,[45] O'Donovan expands on the relationship between character and action, subject to two stipulations—that our acts do not define our character, and yet we shall be known by our acts ('fruits'). Contra the first stipulation, modern ethics is substantially act-ethics, and dispositions of character are reduced to the evidence of repetitive actions; however there are dispositions of character not easily reduced to actions—for example, 'maturity', or 'even-temperedness', or 'lack of initiative'. In relation to the second stipulation, actions have epistemological priority over character; however character is only helpful in understanding a person's actions retrospectively, since character is not fixed, and legitimately varies between people (consistent with the different gifts and callings). Character is a category useful for moral evaluation, rather than moral deliberation, as a category which must remain open until the end of life, and perhaps even until the end of time.

We now come to the second key passage in the examination of the Christian understanding of the respective significance of motive and action—Jesus' primary ethical teaching in the Sermon on the Mount. Again, it is motive (or the outcome of what is in the heart) that is the source, and the ethical equivalent, of the resulting action. This has always seemed very hard teaching.

Christian ethicists have agonised about how seriously to take Jesus' apparent equating of lust with adultery, or anger with murder, and preachers frequently avoid (or fudge over) this core of Jesus' ethical teaching on the grounds of pastoral difficulty. Stassen and Gushee deal with this challenge by framing Jesus' teaching in the Sermon on the Mount as a series of fourteen ethical triads,[46] illustrated in the cases of adultery/lust and murder/anger as follows (Figure 3):

---

45. O'Donovan, *Resurrection and Moral Order*, 206–225.
46. Glen H Stassen and David P Gushee, *Kingdom Ethics: Following Jesus in Contemporary Context* (Downers Grove: InterVarsity Press, 2003), 125–145.

Figure 3 Examples of Stassen & Gushee Ethical Triads in Jesus' Ethical Teaching

	Adultery/Lust (Mt 5:27–30)	Murder/Anger (Mt 5:21–26)
Traditional Righteousness	You shall not commit adultery	You shall not kill
Vicious Cycle	Looking with lust is adultery in the heart	Being angry, or saying, you fool!
Transforming Initiative	Remove the cause of temptation	Go, be reconciled

Their very appealing argument is that the key emphasis in each triad is on the 'transforming initiative', whereas the stumbling-block for many interpreters has stemmed from seeing the 'vicious cycle' as the core of the teaching. This argument is appealing, in that it removes this core of Jesus' teaching from the realm of the apparently impossibly idealistic.[47] But from the perspective of our discussion here, the driver of the transforming initiative is an act of the will, deriving from a renewal of the attitude of the heart, and then evidenced by the resulting actions. Only if the heart is renewed and transformed can the will enable and empower the action of the transforming initiative.

---

47. In an influential commentary, Bruner terms the three elements of the triad 'Old Commandment', 'New Command' and 'Little Steps of Obedience', which implies he sees the 'New Command' (Stassen & Gushee's 'Vicious Cycle') as the core of Jesus' teaching. However Bruner acknowledges the insight from Stassen, implying minimal difference between them in practice, though Bruner would differ in principle from Stassen and Gushee, who see the 'Transforming Initiative' as the core of Jesus' teaching:

> The 'Little Steps' are often unjustly neglected in the wake of the astonishing power and novelty of Jesus' New Command. But they help by giving creative, practical suggestions on how concretely to try to live Jesus' road-clearing new way. Frederick D Bruner, *Matthew: A Commentary Volume 1: The Christbook: Matthew 1-12* (Grand Rapids: Eerdmans, 2004/1987), 207

We have focused in this discussion of the ethical basis of the gospel on the primary relevant statements of Jesus in the gospels. Before leaving this discussion, we touch on a couple of examples from the New Testament letter writers, which reflect the positions on action and motivation with varying degrees of emphasis.

Paul, dealing with the problem of the inconsistency of his desire to serve God contrasted with the sinful actions resulting from his human fallenness, which is the external evidence of an inner conflict, sees his redemption through Christ:

> So I find it to be a law that when I want to do what is good, evil lies close at hand. For I delight in the law of God in my innermost self, but I see in my members another law at war with the law of my mind, making me captive to the law that dwells in my members. Wretched man that I am! Who will rescue me from the body of this death? Thanks be to God, through Jesus Christ our Lord! (Rom 7:21–25a).

Thus, for Paul, motives matter supremely, because it is only by belief in God's grace and forgiveness through Christ that we can be saved, just as it is impossible for us to please God by our actions alone. The inner conflict between the 'law in the mind' and the 'law in the members/body' seems to be Paul's description of the ongoing battle for inner transformation of the heart, as his renewed mind fights to control his wayward actions.

James, dealing with the problem of believers who thought they had no need to concern themselves with good actions, sees good actions as evidence of the transformation within of the innermost motives, expressed as 'faith':

> . . . faith by itself, if it has no works, is dead. But someone will say, 'You have faith and I have works.' Show me your faith apart from your works, and I by my works will show you my faith (Jas 2:17–18).

To summarise, we have focused most attention on Jesus' reinforcement of the two great commandments, and their implications for Christian ethics, particularly our question of the relationship between motive and action. We have also looked briefly at the implications of Jesus' key ethical teaching in the Sermon on the Mount, and even more briefly at selected excerpts from Paul's and James's letters as samples of the variety of New Testament thought on the question (aside from that of the gospel writers—especially focusing on the words they record Jesus using).

The primary conclusion is that consistently throughout the New Testament, what we have termed motive and its wellspring are the primary theological concern, while actions are seen as a consequence of the inner transformation.[48] A variety of terms are used in the New Testament to address the concepts involved, and we have explored the two most important of them—love (*agapē*) and heart (*kardia*) in some detail. There is considerable diversity of opinion on their appropriateness as the key expressions of this wellspring of motives, but none challenges the primary conclusion that motives as such remain central.

The Invisible Hand Tradition in Economics and a Christian Response

With the foregoing discussion of the differing understandings of action and motive in economic and Christian thought as background, it is useful to illustrate this major difference between the two traditions by reference to 'invisible hand' mechanisms.

There is a long-standing tradition in economics, particularly stimulated by the work of Adam Smith, of interest in institutional arrangements where the so-called 'invisible hand' mechanism produces desirable results. The central idea of this metaphor[49] is that good social outcomes can emerge from certain well-designed institutions, without the goodness of those outcomes depending on the behaviour of the participating agents. The special 'virtue' of such institutions

---

48. The initial action may precede as a result of reluctant obedience, but hopefully that inner transformation takes over (or at least begins) and the subsequent obedience becomes less reluctant; hence the process may be more a progressive cycle of transformation and action.
49. There is considerable debate on the precise nature of the expression (see, for example, Warren J Samuels (with assistance from Marianne F Johnson and William H Perry), *Erasing the Invisible Hand: Essays on an Elusive and Misused Concept in Economics*: (Cambridge: Cambridge University Press, 2011) 60–77). However metaphor seems the most reasonable general description, without denying some of the more significant but limited alternatives.

where the invisible hand metaphor is a dominant description ('invisible hand institutions'), is that they make minimal demands for their good operation (and in the limit, no demands at all) on the virtue of participants. Since virtue is scarce among humanity, social arrangements that secure good outcomes without relying on human virtue are prima facie desirable.[50] Invisible hand institutions 'economise on virtue'[51] or 'economise on love'.[52]

In all his writings Smith only uses the invisible hand metaphor three times; two of those are of direct interest to economists, and are somewhat peripheral to his main argument in each of the cases where he uses it. In *The Theory of Moral Sentiments* he seems to be making a rather exaggerated argument of the 'trickle down' variety; he says of the rich:

> They consume little more than the poor, and in spite of their natural selfishness and rapacity . . . they divide with the poor the produce of all their improvements. They are led by an invisible hand to make nearly the same distribution of the necessaries of life, which would have been made, had the earth been divided into equal portions among all its inhabitants, and thus without intending it, advance the interest of the society . . .[53]

A more modest statement of his argument (minus the hyperbole) is that spending by the rich gives employment to the poor, thereby making the distribution of income, particularly on the 'necessaries of life', less unequal, and therefore more amenable to free markets.

In *The Wealth of Nations* Smith argues that the concern of a businessman for his own security and gain leads him to favour domestic rather than foreign investment, to the probable, but on his part, unintentional, benefit of the whole of society:

---

50. And while such actions might be desirable from a Christian perspective also, they would be a great deal better if they arose from good motives.
51. Geoffrey Brennan and Alan Hamlin, *Democratic Devices and Desires* (Cambridge: Cambridge University Press, 2000), chapter 4.
52. Dennis H Robertson, 'What Does the Economist Economize?' (1954), reprinted in his *Economic Commentaries* (London: Staples Press, 1956).
53. Adam Smith, *The Theory of Moral Sentiments* (Cambridge: Cambridge University Press, 2002/1759), Part IV, 215.

By preferring the support of domestic to that of foreign industry, he intends only his own security; and by directing that industry in such a manner as its produce may be of the greatest value, he intends only his own gain, and he is in this, as in many other cases, led by an invisible hand to promote an end which was no part of his intention. Nor is it always worse for the society that he was no part of it. By pursuing his own interest he frequently promotes that of the society more effectually than when he really intends to promote it.[54]

While the first of these direct examples of the invisible hand in Smith is, on the face of it, somewhat questionable, and the second somewhat limited in application,[55] economists have generally attributed to Smith the origination of what has become a wide applicability of the 'invisible hand' in economic institutions. Their standard example of an invisible hand institution is the freely operating market, often citing Smith's memorable statement:

> In civilized society, he [man] stands at all times in need of the cooperation and assistance of great multitudes, while his whole life is scarce sufficient to retain the friendship of a few persons . . . Man has almost constant occasion for the help of his brethren, and it is in vain for him to expect it from their benevolence only. He will be more likely to prevail if he can interest their self-love in his favour and shew them that it is for their own advantage to do for him what he requires of them . . . It is in this manner that we obtain from one another the far greater part of those good offices which we stand in need of. It is not from the benevolence of the butcher, the brewer or the baker that we expect our dinner, but from their regard to their own interest. We address ourselves not to their humanity but to their self-love and never talk of our own necessities but of their advantages.[56]

Smith had spent the first three chapters of his *magnum opus* explaining just how extensive are the gains from specialisation (the 'division of labour'), and hence the huge potential gains from human coop-

---

54. Adam Smith, *The Wealth of Nations*, Volume 1 (Books I-III), Volume 2 (Books IV,V), (London: Penguin, 1999/1776), Book IV, 32.
55. Though in *The Wealth of Nations* example, he acknowledges the applicability of the invisible hand in 'many other [unspecified] cases'.
56. Smith, *The Wealth of Nations*, 118f.

eration on a large scale.⁵⁷ But he sees that the mobilisation of those gains depend on the possibility of exchange, so each individual can satisfy needs and wants by exchange rather than through the limiting and significantly less efficient process of self-sufficiency. People will be led to specialise more extensively if it is in their interests to do so. That is what exchange allows: it encourages each participant in the trading relationship to act in the interests of others even when he has no concern for those others' interests other than instrumentally as a by-product in the pursuit of his own.

Asked what is the fundamental concept in economics, one might offer a variety of suggestions: scarcity, competition, the allocation of resources, optimisation, self-interest. These are all good answers in their own ways, but there is another possible answer that is in many ways better still. This is Smith's answer—the basic concept is 'human cooperation' and the huge material advantages that such cooperation delivers. But the cooperation Smith envisages is not effected psychologically, in that a cooperative spirit *may* be present, but the cooperation does not depend on it. Rather, it depends on a system of mutually agreeable exchanges, in which it may be presumed self-interest is predominant. The cooperation in question can thus be described as 'invisible', though 'not necessarily intentional' is probably more descriptive.

Smith does not presume that all individual market exchanges need to be dominated by self-interest. For example, if the baker feels benevolence for those of his customers who are penurious, and if as a result he decides to supply bread to the hungry where no payment is forthcoming, this would not make it impossible for the market system to operate. Smith's claim seems to have two aspects: first, the analytic claim that the market does not require benevolence for its operation; and second, the empirical claim that, as a matter of fact, most market participants seem not to be driven primarily by benevolence. Some versions of invisible hand reasoning might actually require self-interest,⁵⁸ but Smith's does not seem to. The market,

---

57. Smith, *The Wealth of Nations*, Book I, Chapters I-III.
58. Arguably Mandeville's in *The Fable of the Bees*, Bernard Mandeville *The Fable of the Bees or Private Vices, Publick Benefits*, Vol. 1 (Clarendon Press. 1732), or Hayek's defence of market prices as indicators of marginal value. See Friedrich A von Hayek, 'The Use of Knowledge in Society' in *American Economic Review*, 35(4) (1945): 519–530.

on Smith's view, does not *require* greed: the market is substantially 'motive independent'.

Thus for Smith, it is the well-structured market which makes the benefits of cooperation through specialisation available, and not self-interest as such. Indeed, he gives several examples of the disadvantages of self-interest in the absence of a well-structured market, including from his own field of academia. He cites certain universities in which the professors' remuneration largely depends on fees paid by the students, in which cases the professors have an incentive to attend diligently to the quality of their teaching. By contrast, in universities where professors' remuneration comes directly from central university funds or foundations, there is no such incentive to provide quality instruction, and teaching standards are poor. The self-interested academic who is 'naturally active' has an incentive to 'employ that activity in any way from which he can derive some advantage, rather than in the performance of his duty, from which he can derive none'.[59] Even where teaching standards are supposed to be monitored by other academics who also have, or ought to have, teaching duties, Smith says that, because of self-interest, 'they are likely to make a common cause, to be all very indulgent to one another . . .'[60]

A second point to note is that there is no suggestion in *The Wealth of Nations*—or in the idea of an invisible hand mechanism more generally—that it produces or increases greed (or material motives more broadly).[61] Further, while it is generally argued by neoclassical economists that the invisible hand formulation takes human motivations

---

59. Smith is clearly ignoring any non-material aspect of 'advantage' which might result from a sense of satisfaction to the academic in having taught well or performed his duty.
60. Smith, *The Wealth of Nations*, Book V: 349f. Smith is also making a rather personal point here—his own Glasgow University is an example of his first, market-based institution, while Oxford University (where he studied, at Balliol College, from 1740–1746) is an example of his second, centrally funded institution. Of the latter university, where he was doubtless critical of the teaching standards, he goes as far as to say: 'In the university of Oxford, the greater part of the public professors have, for these many years, given up altogether even the pretence of teaching.' Smith, *The Wealth of Nations*, Book V: 350.
61. The concept of the invisible hand was, of course, formulated long before the (relatively) recent application of the insights of psychology in Behavioural Economics, which field is interested in this assumption.

as given, analysis by behavioural economists of *The Theory of Moral Sentiments* concludes Smith saw motivations as variable, though their analysis does not suggest this variability is due to exchange activity as such.[62] And insofar as Smith has anything to say in *The Wealth of Nations* about the effect of markets on motivations, his remarks focus on the possible narrowing effects of specialisation rather than the effects of exchange activity as such (corrupting or otherwise).[63] Indeed, Smith thinks that life in commercial society makes people more attentive to the needs and wants of others, more punctual and more trustworthy (the 'douce commerce' argument). These effects also arise from self-interest: it pays participants in market exchanges to develop these habits and dispositions.[64]

It is clear that for Smith the rise of commercial society and the consequent diffusion of a 'general plenty . . . through all the different

---

62. Nava Ashraf, Colin F Camerer and George Lowenstein, 'Adam Smith, Behavioral Economist', in *Journal of Economic Perspectives*, 19/3 (Summer 2005): 131–145. They conclude as follows: 'Adam Smith's actors in *The Theory of Moral Sentiments* are driven by an internal struggle between their impulsive, fickle and indispensable passions, and the impartial spectator. They weigh out-of-pocket costs more than opportunity costs, have self-control problems and are overconfident. They display erratic patterns of sympathy, but are consistently concerned about fairness and justice. They are motivated more by ego than by any kind of direct pleasure from consumption and, though they don't anticipate it, ultimately derive little pleasure from either. In short, Adam Smith's world is not inhabited by dispassionate rational purely self-interested agents, but rather by multidimensional and realistic human beings.' 'Adam Smith, Behavioral Economist', 142.
63. Smith also notes that commercial society tends to 'extinguish the martial spirit' and makes it difficult for a people to defend themselves. (Smith, *Wealth of Nations*, Book V: 373) But whereas Smith considers this a loss, one might argue that a society lacking the inclination to heroism might also lack the inclination towards military adventurism—peaceability is not obviously a moral inadequacy, even if it is partly a matter of timidity.
64. In the *Lectures on Jurisprudence* Smith remarks that the Dutch are more 'faithfull to their word' than the English, and the English more so than the Scots—and that this is because commercial society is better developed in Holland than in England than in Scotland. Adam Smith, *Lectures on Jurisprudence*, R L Meek, D D Raphael and P G Stein, editors (Oxford: Oxford University Press, 1978/1763), paragraph 327. One might concede Smith's empirical claim but suspect that he got the direction of causation wrong, that is that greater innate trustworthiness is the cause of more developed commercial society rather than vice-versa.

ranks of society'[65] is a good thing. Yet the institution of the market itself is not a matter of deliberate design by humankind.[66]

As regards attempts at management of the market, Smith counsels minimal interference. The only duties of government are protection of society from external invasion, protection of every member of society from injustice or oppression by others, and the creation and maintenance of necessary public goods which would be unprofitable for individuals or small groups of them to provide. To go beyond these necessary functions is to risk overreaching:

> The sovereign is completely discharged from a duty, in the attempting to perform which he must always be exposed to innumerable delusions, and for the proper performance of which no human wisdom or knowledge could ever be sufficient; the duty of superintending the industry of private people, and of directing it towards the employments most suitable to the interest of the society.[67]

In Smith's understanding, the invisible hand of the market not only operates unseen, and without any necessary or overt intention of societal benefit on the part of the participants, but it also originates similarly. Markets may be 'constructed' to meet a perceived social need, but primarily and most usually they emerge spontaneously in response to the obvious and ubiquitous individual (and hence social) benefits of specialisation and exchange. Smith clearly sees this emergence as 'providential' and refers to it as the action of a 'benign deity'—though it is not by any means clear how he intended this reference to be taken, literally or figuratively.[68]

---

65. Smith, *Wealth of Nations*, Book 1, 115.
66. Smith, *Wealth of Nations*, Book 1, Chapter I-III.
67. Smith, *Wealth of Nations*, Book IV, 274.
68. For a debate on precisely this question, see Lisa Hill, 'The Hidden Theology of Adam Smith', in *European Journal of the History of Economic Thought* 8/1 (Spring 2001): 1-29; James E Alvey, 'The hidden theology of Adam Smith: A belated reply to Hill', in *European Journal of the History of Economic Thought*, 11/4 (February 2004): 623-628; Lisa Hill, Lisa 'Further Reflections on the Hidden Theology of Adam Smith', in *European Journal of the History of Economic Thought* 11/4 (February 2004): 629-635.

Smith's personal theological views are not transparent, nor are they relevant to the present argument.[69] The influence on the emerging understanding of the invisible hand metaphor of Smith's personal views and the broader intellectual and social climate of the period, while of some interest, are not fundamental to the argument. What is fundamental is an aspect of the invisible hand notion that is widespread amongst mainstream economists—namely, that invisible hand institutions operate primarily via effects on action, with basic motives and attitudes unaffected.[70] Accordingly, economists' interest in invisible hand mechanisms adopts a normative framework of evaluation in which motives and attitudes do not play the decisive role, since if the primary normative framework focuses on the virtue of agents, then the impact of any 'invisible hand' structure will necessarily be second-order.

It is worth at this point referring more broadly, albeit briefly, to Christian theological thinking relevant to the consideration of the economic doctrine of the invisible hand. Stemming from the fundamental Christian principle of the omnipotent, omniscient, all-loving divine nature,[71] God is understood to undergird the good but fallen creation in the working out of his divine plan of the renewal of creation, including in the case of humanity, (at least) in relation to the

---

69. The question of whether Smith believed there was some element of divine providence in the invisible hand, in the context of the long-standing theological debate on the question of divine providence, raises an interesting subject for comparison of economic and Christian thought. There is quite some literature on the subject of Smith's theological position (see, for example, Paul Oslington, 'God and the Market: Adam Smith's Invisible Hand', in *Journal of Business Ethics*, 108/4 (2012): 429–438 and Brendan Long, 'Adam Smith's Theodicy', in *Adam Smith as Theologian*, edited by Paul Oslington (London: Routledge, 2011), 98–105. However as the theological position taken by Smith (or indeed mainstream subsequent economists qua economic thinkers) is now defined to be outside the economic intellectual discipline, it does not directly bear on the motive/action question from a strictly *economic* perspective.
70. However this is not an uncontroversial issue amongst intellectuals more broadly, particularly in relation to areas of public life formerly regarded as providing common goods, and where markets have previously not operated—for example see Michael Sandel, *What Money Can't Buy: The Moral Limits of Markets* (New York: Farrar, Straus and Giroux, 2012), especially Chapter 3 'How Markets Crowd Out Morals'.
71. Supported by many biblical texts and generally agreed theological discussion—see, for example, Millard J Erickson, *Theology* (Grand Rapids: Baker Book House, 1983), Chapters 16–18.

redeemed elect.[72] Whoever ultimately forms part of the redeemed elect,[73] it seems reasonably clear from scripture and two millennia of theological debate that God's ultimate plan is for their good.[74]

What is more theologically problematic, however, is the place in God's plan of economic institutions such as markets. Does the divine undergirding of creation extend to markets as potential vehicles for human flourishing generally, including the relief of poverty and suffering? Or are markets an integral and fallen part of a fallen world, which must inevitably function in the face of greed? Or, thirdly, are markets, as some argue in relation to guns, ethically neutral, and tools to be used for the difficult task of discriminating between good and evil, according to human motivation and resulting action? Christian writers have adopted all three positions with equal vigour; Atherton summarises the arguments well and quotes from selected leading proponents of each.[75] In his conclusion (written over twenty years ago), Atherton expressed ambivalence about the traditional liberal response of the church, and argued that more direct engagement with both the conservative and radical responses was called for. He

---

72. An example biblical text is Rom 8:28: 'We know that in everything God works for good with those who love him, who are called according to his purpose.'
73. Throughout Christian history there has been considerable theological debate about the extent and qualification of the elect, ranging for example from extreme Calvinist doctrine of 'double predestination' (that is, that God predetermines ahead of time and at an individual level who will be redeemed and who will be damned), to the other extreme of universalism (that is, that all will be saved in the end; there have been many versions of this doctrine throughout Christian history).
74. For a representative contemporary array of theological thought on issues of divine providence, see Francesca A Murphy and Philip G Ziegler, *The Providence of God*, (London/New York: T&T Clark, 2009), especially essays by Katherine Sondregger, 'The Doctrine of Providence' (144–157); and John Webster, 'On the Theology of Providence' (158–175).
75. John Atherton in *Christianity and the Market: Christian Social Thought for Our Times*, (London: SPCK, 1992) summarises the arguments of key Christian writers propounding each view: The Conservative Response. Affirming the Market Economy: The Tradition of Christian Political Economy – substantially based on the writings of Brian Griffiths (85–116); The Radical Response. Rejecting the Market Economy: The Tradition of Christian Socialism—based on a number of writers, particularly Ulrich Duchrow, RH Tawney and FD Maurice (117–155); The Liberal Response. Subordinating the Market: The Mainstream Liberal Tradition – based on a number of writers, particularly J Philip Wogaman and RH Preston (156–192).

has more recently developed these ideas, indicating ways in which Christians and the church generally can engage more directly and positively with a political and economic world which has become more amenable to the conservative position, while seeking to retain important elements from the radical position.[76]

Suffice it to say that, while there remain significant elements of a deep Christian scepticism about the morality of markets, particularly how market participants have behaved recently, and how they have been regulated (for example, during and in the wake of the 2008 Global Financial Crisis), there seems to be a greater recognition by Christian thinkers than was the case thirty or more years ago, that there is no alternative to a constructive engagement with a globalised market economy.

There is likely to be some anxiety, especially but not only amongst thinkers who are also *Christians*, that a social system that is tolerant of self-interest (and in the extreme, greed) will serve to produce more of it. Such thinkers might well argue that it would be preferable if only the virtuous thrive (in the broad sense of the term, and certainly not just financially),[77] since that will provide a general incentive to virtue. Or perhaps, if the virtuous are more likely to survive (and/or reproduce?), some analogue of evolutionary processes may ensure that virtue abounds in society.[78] And if a particular social structure has the effect of detaching virtue from thriving (or from surviving), then so much the worse for that social structure.

---

76. John Atherton, *Transfiguring Capitalism: An Enquiry into Religion and Global Change* (London: SPCK, 2008).
77. A matter of some contention in contemporary Christian discourse is the so-called 'prosperity gospel', the notion that God intends Christians to thrive financially, but which has been the source of considerable financial abuse by preachers espousing the notion, usually of poor people hoping for divine intervention in their financial plight. For discussion see Kate Bowler, *Blessed: A History of the American Prosperity Gospel* (Oxford: Oxford University Press, 2013), and Lausanne Theology Working Group, *A Statement on the Prosperity Gospel*, January 2010. https://www.lausanne.org/content/a-statement-on-the-prosperity-gospel.
78. There is emerging evidence from evolutionary biology that cooperative structures can be sustained under certain conditions of natural selection, with significant ethical implications for societies in which competitive markets dominate. See Martin Nowak and Roger Highfield, *Super Cooperators: Beyond the Survival of the Fittest; Why Cooperation, not Competition, is the Key to Life* (Edinburgh: Canongate, 2011).

If this is so, then the difference between the economic and Christian views of market structures can largely be explained, not in terms of any disagreement about the way in which markets operate, but rather in terms of disagreements as to the content of the rival bases of evaluation. This rivalry is not so much a matter of 'consequentialism' versus 'deontology', but rather of a consequentialism in which different 'consequences' count differently. The Christian focuses primarily on the effects of different social institutional arrangements on the virtue of the agents—on their motives and attitudes.[79] The economist, particularly if an invisible hand enthusiast, is inclined to think that markets, independently of agents' motives and attitudes, matter predominantly instrumentally in terms of producing a more tolerable life, primarily in the efficiency of the provision of material goods, for larger numbers of people.

From a Christian perspective, market mechanisms which provide material benefits independent of any considerations of their impact on the virtue of participants, are desirable as far as they go. But much more desirable are arrangements in which the virtue of participants is or can be enhanced by the market interaction, under the influence of the Holy Spirit. Where the subject becomes problematic, however, is in determining exactly how market mechanisms might be adjusted or managed such that the virtue of participants can be enhanced, while still enabling the provision of material benefits. Frequently such suggested adjustments or management approaches are designed to limit what are seen as the ethical negativities of competition; however of relevance here is Frank Knight's comment that critics of competition 'generally underestimate egregiously the danger of doing vastly worse'.[80]

There is a more nuanced economic response than 'irrelevant!' to the issue of what effects markets have on agents' motives and attitudes. Smith thought that commercial society generated greater trustworthiness, greater attentiveness to the interests of others (albeit largely for self-interested reasons), and a more peaceable disposition (albeit mainly grounded in timidity).[81] He also thought that the

---

79. Though the Christian focus is not exclusive—see the discussion in our first section above.
80. Frank H Knight 'The Ethics of Competition' in *Quarterly Journal of Economics*, 37 (1923): 602.
81. For an extended discussion of this issue see McCloskey, *The Bourgeois Virtues*, on the 'bourgeois virtues'.

division of labour was likely to lead to a more limited preoccupation, to a dullness among the large bulk of the working poor[82]—a misgiving which Marx emphasised in his own interpretation of Smith's account. On balance, Smith, as a recognised member of the 'douce commerce' school, thought the effects of commercial society on the motives and attitudes of its participants are benign—though the argument is not un-nuanced. There are also the potentially negative effects, both ethical and material, of deviation from symmetry between the participants' power in the exchange interaction. But importantly, any such effects were in Smith's view to be balanced by the substantial material benefits accruing from commercial society. For Smith, those material benefits had to be accorded significant weight in any proper assessment.

So far in our discussion the focus has been on the market system as the primary case of an 'invisible hand' mechanism, but it is not the only example. For example economists have over the last fifty years created a significant sub-field in political theory called 'public choice' theory, in which democratic institutions are investigated for their 'invisible hand' properties. The basic idea here is that, despite their protestations of their priority for service of the common good, and accepting that they have a genuine concern for such public service, political operatives in the end are motivated by self-interest. In this context, a central feature of democracy is the provision of constraints on political office-holders that encourage them to act broadly in the interests of the citizenry. Thus one central element in the argument of the apologist for democracy is that elections encourage outcomes that are not too distant from the citizens' collective interests, even

---

82. To quote Smith:

> The man whose whole life is spent in performing a few simple operations, of which the effects are perhaps always the same, has no occasion to exert his understanding or to exercise his invention in finding out expedients for removing difficulties which never occur. He naturally loses, therefore, the habit of such exertion, and generally becomes as stupid and ignorant as it is possible for a human being to become . . . But in every improved and civilised society this is the state into which the labouring poor, that is, the great body of people, must necessarily fall, unless the government takes some pains to prevent it. (Smith, *Wealth of Nations*, Book V: 368f)

Consequently, Smith's recommendations for government action in the provision of education follow from this anxiety.

when the political representatives' inclinations might be otherwise.[83] Or as Hamilton put it, democracy serves to bend the politician's interests to the service of duty—which he regarded as 'the best security for the fidelity of mankind'.[84] Undoubtedly this social safeguard does not offer an ethically flattering view of politicians; neither does the invisible hand perspective offer an ethically flattering view of market agents. But in the light of the doctrine of human fallenness, a Christian might well argue that this is no bad thing, in that it leads to a lively sense of human moral inadequacy and the need of redemption. Further it would arguably be an over-optimistic feature of social organisation if agents could plausibly maintain that their thriving (whether economically or politically) reflected their relative virtue!

Of course, no such thought has been central to economists. The first and foremost thought is that relations among persons (political and economic) should be structured to secure the best material outcomes for them: the invisible hand perspective is in that sense resolutely 'action-oriented'.

The concept of a common good transcending the sum of individual goods does not seem to fit here. Of course the arguably greater likelihood of oppression or exploitation (at least of minorities) when the task of determining the common good is left in the hands of parliament or a 'benign' dictator might well lead to the conclusion that the economic understanding is that most consistent with a bitterly realistic view of human nature. But the sometime idealism of Christians who, dreaming of the eschatological rule of Christ in the renewed creation, and perhaps indulging nostalgia for an optimistically viewed and long-departed Christendom, can be seduced by an overly optimistic view of the potential for democracy and human leadership. What the strand of economic thought discussed here can show Christians is a more realistic view of human institutions, institutions that can sometimes galvanise them into positive social action, perhaps even suggestive of the Kingdom.

---

83. Of course, citizens' perceptions of their interests may differ from a more rational (often longer term) view of reality—and thus electoral structures are not particularly encouraging of 'visionary leadership'. However, the argument is in the spirit of Churchill's famous observation that democracy is the worst of system of government, except for the others! (And this from a politician whose taste for 'visionary leadership' was considerable!)
84. Alexander Hamilton, *Federalist, No. 72*, 1788. http://press-pubs.uchicago.edu/founders/documents/a2_1_1s15.html

Conclusion

The central presupposition of this paper is that some progress in the communication between Christianity and economics—whether thought of as academic disciplines or simply as 'approaches' to the questions that concern them—can be achieved if each has a good sense of 'where the other is coming from'. And our central claim is that one significant difference between the Christianity and economics is the normative framework that each employs.

We do not want to make excessive claims in this regard: the differences are matters of relative weight rather than categorical exclusion. But it does seem clear that economics is considerably more focused on actions and that Christianity is more focused on motives and attitudes (without being indifferent to actions)—and that this difference helps to explain why economists and Christian theologians or ethicists often talk past one another when they consider what looks like the same subject matter. So in particular, when economists talk of broad institutional arrangements like the market or democratic politics—or more detailed arrangements such as monopoly or the separation of powers or federal structures or fixed terms for political representatives – they will look to the ways in which those arrangements impact on the actions that agents take and the resultant outcomes that are produced under the arrangement. The Christian tradition tends to be more interested in questions of how such institutional arrangements influence the motives and attitudes of those involved,[85] with the actions consequential upon those motives and attitudes being of secondary (albeit often still important) concern.

But being alert to the distinction can do work as well within both economics and Christianity as separate disciplines. Whether the issue is one of normative social theory or biblical interpretation, the distinction between action effects and motive/attitude effects is worth bearing in mind. That distinction rests of course on the claim that such a distinction can plausibly be made. For economists, it is a routine distinction (as the 'invisible hand' analysis exemplifies). Other disciplines, including Christian theology/ethics, are perhaps more prone to 'attribution errors'—to assuming an overly close association between motive and action, at least in some contexts. Economists

---

85. Or perhaps what those institutional arrangements themselves express in terms of values.

do not, of course, deny that motives/attitudes influence behaviour, but much of their explanatory energy is focused on ways in which changes in behaviour can be wrought without requiring any change in underlying motives or attitudes. Perhaps in each discipline there is an excessive tendency to focus on one of action or motive to the exclusion of the other.

At the normative level, perhaps the aim should be an appropriate synthesis of action and motive/attitude elements into an overarching framework in which all are appropriately weighed. Perhaps agreement on the parameters of such a framework is a necessary condition for establishing a justification for any serious conversation between economists and Christians (and more generally between social scientists and Christians). All serious conversation presupposes that there are things that each can learn from the other. But serious conversation also presupposes enough common understanding that participants are not consigned to endless talking at cross-purposes.

Printed by Libri Plureos GmbH in Hamburg, Germany